Editor-in-Chief and Founder:
Lyndon H. LaRouche, Jr.
Editorial Board: *Lyndon H. LaRouche, Jr. , Helga Zepp-LaRouche, Robert Ingraham, Tony Papert, Gerald Rose, Dennis Small, Jeffrey Steinberg, William Wertz*
Co-Editors: *Robert Ingraham, Tony Papert*
Managing Editor: *Nancy Spannaus*
Technology: *Marsha Freeman*
Books: *Katherine Notley*
Ebooks: *Richard Burden*
Graphics: *Alan Yue*
Photos: *Stuart Lewis*
Circulation Manager: *Stanley Ezrol*

INTELLIGENCE DIRECTORS
Counterintelligence: *Jeffrey Steinberg, Michele Steinberg*
Economics: *John Hoefle, Marcia Merry Baker, Paul Gallagher*
History: *Anton Chaitkin*
Ibero-America: *Dennis Small*
Russia and Eastern Europe: *Rachel Douglas*
United States: *Debra Freeman*

INTERNATIONAL BUREAUS
Bogotá: *Miriam Redondo*
Berlin: *Rainer Apel*
Copenhagen: *Tom Gillesberg*
Houston: *Harley Schlanger*
Lima: *Sara Madueño*
Melbourne: *Robert Barwick*
Mexico City: *Gerardo Castilleja Chávez*
New Delhi: *Ramtanu Maitra*
Paris: *Christine Bierre*
Stockholm: *Ulf Sandmark*
United Nations, N.Y.C.: *Leni Rubinstein*
Washington, D.C.: *William Jones*
Wiesbaden: *Göran Haglund*

ON THE WEB
e-mail: eirns@larouchepub.com
www.larouchepub.com
www.executiveintelligencereview.com
www.larouchepub.com/eiw
Webmaster: *John Sigerson*
Assistant Webmaster: *George Hollis*
Editor, Arabic-language edition: *Hussein Askary*

EIR (ISSN 0273-6314) *is published weekly (50 issues), by EIR News Service, Inc., P.O. Box 17390, Washington, D.C. 20041-0390. (703) 297-8434*

European Headquarters: E.I.R. GmbH, Postfach Bahnstrasse 9a, D-65205, Wiesbaden, Germany
Tel: 49-611-73650
Homepage: http://www.eir.de
e-mail: info@eir.de
Director: Georg Neudecker

Montreal, Canada: 514-461-1557
eir@eircanada.ca

Denmark: EIR - Danmark, Sankt Knuds Vej 11, basement left, DK-1903 Frederiksberg, Denmark.
Tel.: +45 35 43 60 40, Fax: +45 35 43 87 57. e-mail: eirdk@hotmail.com.

Mexico City: EIR, Sor Juana Inés de la Cruz 242-2 Col. Agricultura C.P. 11360
Delegación M. Hidalgo, México D.F.
Tel. (5525) 5318-2301
eirmexico@gmail.com

Canada Post Publication Sales Agreement #40683579

Postmaster: Send all address changes to *EIR*, P.O. Box 17390, Washington, D.C. 20041-0390.

Signed articles in *EIR* represent the views of the authors, and not necessarily those of the Editorial Board.

Crush the Coup Plotters

EDITORIAL

This Is Not the Time for Con-Artist Tricks or Nazi Schemes

by Robert Ingraham

June 12—The catastrophic crisis descending upon the people of New York City has now placed—front-and-center—the immediate challenge of how that crisis, and similar urgencies throughout the nation, must be resolved. Nothing that has been proposed so far by a wide array of government leaders, to address the escalating breakdown of the New York transit system, will work under the existing axioms of financial policy making. Much of what has been proposed are outright fraudulent schemes dreamed up by financial con-artists. In truth, the actual solution is not to be found in New York City, *per se*, but rather, in the necessary requirement for a dramatic change in U.S. national economic and financial policy.

None of what New Yorkers are now facing was inevitable. It was the frame-up of Lyndon LaRouche between 1986 and 1989, his incarceration in a federal penitentiary from 1989 to 1994, and then the restrictions of his extended parole, which led directly to the takeover of U.S. economic and financial policy by the sharks of London and Wall Street, as well as to the subsequent destruction of the productive economy of the United States and the ongoing and escalating immiseration of the American people. It was Lyndon LaRouche, and the national organization he created, who stood in the way, blocking the intended economic rape of America, and it was the jailing of LaRouche which led directly to the repeal of Glass-Steagall, the legalization of derivatives financial gambling, and to a national policy of de-industrialization.

Lyndon LaRouche has repeatedly, and succinctly,

put forward a rigorous approach for overcoming this crisis. His 2014 statement, "Four New Laws to Save the U.S.A. Now!" provides a Hamiltonian solution to this crisis, one guaranteed to work. It is the utter failure of U.S. political leaders and policy makers—as well as of the American people—to take up those Four Laws, which has now created a situation in which nothing that is being proposed will succeed. The expression, "LaRouche's Four Laws," is not a slogan. It is not a campaign "tactic." It is the only economic and banking policy which will work.

The fundamental issue, the inescapable issue at hand, is the proper role of the National Government in economic and financial policy making. Since LaRouche's 1989 jailing, the U.S. government has uniformly abdicated its Constitutional responsibility, and control over the nation's fortunes have been turned over to the designs of "deregulated" financial interests, many of whom have acted to deliberately destroy both the productive potential of the nation and the well-being of the people.

Today, we urgently need a lawful policy for the national issuance of large amounts of Federal public credit to finance the reconstruction and development of the nation's infrastructure and productive economy. This is required *now!* It cannot wait any longer.

The Wise Words of Lyndon LaRouche

On June 12, in a discussion with some of his associates that centered on the transit crisis in New York City, Lyndon LaRouche had a good deal to say. We present here edited excerpts of what he had to say.

LaRouche: There *is* no government fund. There *is* no solid government funding in the United States. There is none. That's the point! Manhattan itself could go entirely deep, deep, deep. Suddenly. Why? Because there was no substance to the [financial] paper that they created—without value, without any evidence, without any content. ... and they cannot possibly produce anything, which means that the whole thing is going to sink; and Manhattan could sink, not actually but financially.

Without [government financing] there is no possibility of saving this part of the economy. The federal government leads and puts those things on the table, and then you might be able to get something out.

The federal government should be taking over, ... as a security for this business, because only the federal government has the authority to develop sufficient backing for the process. Then you might find something. But if someone is trying to say, "I've got something in my backdoor, and I can open the door," that's *suicide* and stupidity. You've got to get the federal government of the United States to actually assume an orderly form of credit for an active practice. That's the only way this thing can be done. Paper dreams do not produce anything. They're doing a "non-production." Everything they say they are doing now is a fraud, because there is no track of any evidence of an actual funding; and that's the problem.

The core of this thing is the Nazis, is a Nazi-like system, and it's fairly described as a new Nazi system.

Question: Is this financial policy of destroying the United States inherently a Nazi policy?

LaRouche: It would have to be; otherwise, it wouldn't work. That's what the situation is there. People get stuck into wishful beliefs in things that will never come true, and that's what it is. The only way we can get something which will solve the problem is to use the Federal organization, through a public issue [of credit]. That will do it. Without that, no!

Question: You have people around President Trump trying to get him away from the American System policy he was referring to recently. Now there are people who are trying to get him away from that. Is that what you would say?

LaRouche: Exactly. Exactly. The right people in Manhattan have already understood this. You've got to look at the whole thing. Currently, there is no answer, there is no guaranteed equity for the entire system of the United States. None! This was done by the former FBI, which ran this operation.

If you're going to save the nation, you're going to have to have a responsible posting, which puts on the table a use of funds for the whole nation. It can be done. It can be done, and with some in this world as a whole, we can do that.

All you have to do is have an agreement within the United States and the government operating on the basis of its commitment to a necessary investment. *That's what's needed!*

Without that, all dreams are dead.

LaRouche: Stop the FBI Fraud!
Stop the Coup Against President Trump!

EDITORIAL

June 8—Lyndon LaRouche has called upon the American people to shut down the coup underway against President Trump, which was fed today by the lying testimony of fired FBI Director James Comey before the Senate Select Committee on Intelligence. LaRouche said that the coup is an FBI-type operation attempting to destroy the United States, and if it is not stopped, the world will face general warfare.

On June 7, former Director of National Intelligence (DNI) James Clapper revealed the actual motivation for the coup against Trump in remarks in Australia. He said that Trump's openness to peace with Russia—the platform upon which Trump was elected by the American people—was itself wholly against U.S. national security interests, in effect, equivalent to treason. It was already known in official Washington, well before the election, that President Obama, in collusion with the British, candidate Clinton, DNI Clapper, CIA Director John Brennan, and FBI Director James Comey, had steered the United States onto a war course with Russia and China, which was meant to be fully activated with Clinton's election.

Trump was elected instead, triggering the coup which has followed. President Trump has kept his promise and established better relations with both Russia and China, who are seeking cooperation with the United States in developing the world, based on great infrastructure projects. That is the only issue here. Comey backed that up Thursday in a long rant against Russia as a mortal enemy, in response to a question from Senator Joe Manchin.

Comey Admits Tasking to Entrap Trump

Here's how the actual conspiracy worked in general outline. According to Comey's own words and their actual implication, on January 6, two weeks before Trump's inauguration, FBI Director Comey is selected by Obama's intelligence chiefs to do a "J. Edgar Hoover" on Trump, briefing him on salacious blackmail material fabricated by British intelligence and Clinton campaign operative Christopher Steele. It is a pure Hoover blackmail operation.

Comey signals to Trump, "give up your fantasy about cooperation with Russia and we won't release this." Trump doesn't budge. The very next day the whole Steele dossier is leaked all over the international news media, accusing the President-elect of perverse sexual acts with Russian hookers. Comey admitted as much in his testimony June 8, saying he was aware that that briefing could be construed as a "J. Edgar Hoover moment," in response to a question from Senator Susan Collins of Maine.

During his meeting with the President, Comey assures him that he is not under FBI investigation. Comey goes out and writes a classified memo about the briefing and the President's responses. Was this memo shared with the British? Who else was it shared with?

Comey claims that he wrote it up because he thought the President would lie about the meeting. That is hogwash. Comey had already been tasked to bring down the President, to entrap him, if Trump did not back down on seeking better relations with Russia and China. That James Comey set out to entrap the President, is the only logical conclusion which can be drawn from Comey's testimony in response to questions by various Republican Senators.

First, Senator James Risch:

Risch: I remember, you talked with us shortly after February 14th, when the *New York Times* wrote an article that suggested that the Trump campaign was colluding with the Russians ... that report by the *New York*

Times was not true. Is that a fair statement?

Comey: In the main it was not true.

With respect to the alleged Michael Flynn conversation:

Risch: You quoted exactly what the President said, "I hope you can see your way clear to letting this go, to letting Flynn go. He is a good guy. I hope you can let this go." … He didn't direct you to let it go?

Comey: Not in his words, no.

Risch: He didn't order you to let it go?

Comey: Again, those words are not an order.

Risch: You don't know of anyone being charged for hoping something?

Comey: I don't as I sit here.

In any truthful scenario that should have ended the matter right there.

No Obstruction of Justice

Various Republican senators asked Comey repeatedly, why, if the President had asked for his loyalty and had told him to drop the Flynn investigation (which was a false statements investigation that the President in all probability did not even know about), why did he not report it to the Attorney General? Alternatively, why did he not threaten to resign, as he had done previously in a confrontation with President George W. Bush? Why keep meeting with the President, telling the President he was not under investigation, while refusing to tell the public the same thing, and returning to strategize with FBI agents about what was said and what were the next steps?

Comey admitted, during his testimony, that he did not do certain logical things, including telling the President to stop any improper conduct, because the FBI had decided that these conversations were of "investi-gative interest," that is, Comey, acting as an undercover informant, had not yet succeeded in completely setting up President Trump.

Comey included Assistant FBI Director Andrew McCabe in the circle of people he was briefing on all of his interchanges with the President. Unfortunately for Comey and this entire "obstruction of justice" scenario, McCabe testified under oath to Congress on May 11, following all of these events, that there had been no effort by Trump or anyone else to interfere with or obstruct the FBI investigation. In fact, Comey himself, in his June 8 Senate testimony, said that prior to his firing, there was no investigation of President Trump for either obstruction of justice or collusion with the Russians.

End This Coup Attempt!

In a statement following Comey's staged performance, President Trump's lawyer, Marc Kasowitz, denied that the President ever asked Comey to let the Michael Flynn matter go, ever pressured Comey, or ever asked for Comey's "loyalty." Kasowitz appropriately emphasized these parts of Comey's testimony:

• The alleged Russian hacking did not change any votes.

• The President told Comey that if any of his satellite associates did something wrong, it would be good to find that out.

• James Comey admitted that he leaked all of his memos about his conversations with President Trump to the *New York Times*, in order to provoke the appointment of a special prosecutor. At least one of these memos was classified.

This is not a battle that will go to court. Whether it continues or not is a question for the American people and their representatives. As LaRouche said, it is time for the people to speak and end this disruptive and highly dangerous, attempted coup. It is also time for the coup plotters to be investigated, including the treasonous news media.

EIR Contents

www.larouchepub.com Volume 44, Number 24, June 16, 2017

CC/Laurie Nevay-IMG

Cover This Week

The MI6 Building at Vauxhall Cross, London. The building also houses the headquarters of the British Secret Intelligence Service (SIS).

I. Sylvia Olden Lee (June 29, 1917 – April 10, 2004)

DR. SIMON ESTES

Uplifting and Educating Young Minds through Classical Music

On June 4, Lynn Yen, the Executive Director of the Foundation for the Revival of Classical Culture, interviewed the world renowned artist Simon Estes. A video of that interview may be found here. On June 29, both Mr. Estes and Ms. Yen will be participating in the "Tribute to Sylvia Olden Lee" at Carnegie Hall in New York City. This event, organized as a Centennial Celebration Concert in honor of Sylvia Olden Lee, is sponsored by the Foundation for the Revival of Classical Culture, in collaboration with the Schiller Institute and the Harlem Opera Theater. The website for the event may be found here.

Lynn Yen: Hello, my name is Lynn Yen. I'm the Executive Director of the Foundation for the Revival of Classical Culture. I'm here with Dr. Simon Estes, who is one of the most renowned opera singers in the world. He has a career spanning more than five decades; in fact he's going into the 58th year of his musical career. He's sung in over eighty-four opera houses in the world; he has sung in front of more than one hundred orchestras, six presidents, the pope, and other international figures, including Presidents Johnson, Nixon, Carter, Clinton and Obama, as well as Desmond Tutu and Nelson Mandela, on and on and on. We will be having a concert, featuring Dr. Estes, a concert in tribute to a great vocal coach, Sylvia Olden Lee, on June 29, and the concert will involve an audience, we hope, of more than one thousand young people from all over New York City.

Dr. Estes, I have a few questions for you regarding

US Department of Agriculture

Dr. Simon Estes

education. The first is, what do you think about education for youth in classical music, and how did you become interested in it? I know you have a foundation...

Dr. Simon Estes: Right. It is vitally important that young people are introduced to classical music at a very young age. Not only is it something that will motivate the talents that many of them have that they don't know they have; but also we know that when children are introduced at a young age to classical music, that generally speaking, they do better academically in school and they are involved in far fewer problems of juvenile delinquency. So it is vitally important for young people to get involved in classical music.

Lynn Yen: Your first vocal teacher was quite an amazing individual.

Dr. Estes: He was. He is still alive; he's 90 years of age, Charles Kellis, and I believe God sent him to the University of Iowa in 1961 to discover me. That's how important I tell young people the teachers are, in many different other areas. Teachers are there because they want to educate us; and this man knew about classical music and opera, and he said, 'you have a voice to sing opera.' I had never heard of opera in my life. So without this teacher (young people remember that!), teachers are vitally important and so is education.

Yen: You were 18 or 20?
Estes: No! The first time I started working with Mr. Kellis I was 23.

Yen: Wow!
Estes: That is the first time I was ever introduced to classical music.

Yen: Amazing; that's wonderful! My second question is what is the difference between classical music in Europe and the United States, or the United States compared to other countries?

Estes: First of all, most classical music, even pre-Baroque, then Baroque or Classical periods, then the Romantic period, most of this music was composed in European countries by Europeans, so they have had a longer history of this type of music, especially in terms of performing it, than the United States, because so many of those composers were over four hundred years

> "If you think of all the symphonies—and Sylvia knew most of them—as well as music with text, a person can create within their own imagination and their emotion, and their heart will be touched to appreciate this type of music. I think it is vitally important that it should be included in the educational curriculum in the elementary schools up through the high schools."

ago, and the United States is very young. So it has been vitally important in the field of classical music.

Yen: Right, exactly. I know you told us, and Sylvia Olden Lee's grandfather was born a slave on the Olden plantation, escaped to the North and joined the Union Army, and your grandfather was also born a slave. And you said there's a sales paper of $500?
Estes: My grandfather was sold for $500, born in Virginia in 1837…

Yen: That's amazing.
Estes: …and here I am, somewhat free and an opera singer.

Yen: And you've sung in the major opera houses, all the major opera houses throughout world. What has provided you with the inspiration to do what you do, and have a life so very different and so vastly…

Estes: I have to say, it really goes back to Charles Kellis, the man who introduced me to classical music. I knew nothing about opera; he loaned me recordings of famous opera singers and a symphonic recording also, so that I would have experience with this type of music, which I had not had any exposure to. That's why I think it is vitally important that young people, at a young age, get exposure to classical music, because I think inside of probably 90 percent of them they will love this type of music, and it will be healthy for them.

Yen: That's beautiful. That leads to the question, what do you think about the capability of classical music to provide emotional education for people, especially when it comes to the issues of rage and violence which are often a big problem in the United States today.

Estes: I think if young people go to more music appreciation courses—I know a lot of schools have dropped that from the curriculum—but I think they need to have exposure to this type of music, to sing and to play classical instruments. And they have to be very careful at which age to begin. If they want to be a pianist or a violinist, for example, they must start at a very young age: three, four, five years. If you're going to sing opera you have to be very, very careful, because your vocal chords are still developing in the body. So I believe Sylvia always wanted young people to have patience, especially if they wanted to sing classical music.

Yen: Right. She had this thing called Saving Young Lyric Voices In Advance, Project SYLVIA, and we intend to ensure the proper technique, bel canto, and at the proper pitch, the Verdi pitch, so that it can be done right.

Estes: Because Verdi knew what he wanted!

Yen: Verdi knew what he was doing!
Estes: That's right!

Yen: Do you have any suggestions as to how musical education should proceed in the United States today, and also what do you think about the need to create a new audience for classical music, because we all know it's getting to be more older people in the audience.

Estes: I think it needs to start in the elementary school. I really do. Young people have a short span of concentration, but I think if they were to play some beautiful music by Schubert, or Brahms or Beethoven or Bach or Verdi or Puccini, and get the right type of music for them to hear for the first time, they will like it. For example, symphonic music; most of it doesn't have text. Giuseppe Verdi wrote that the drama is in the music. So the music is vitally important.

If you think of all the symphonies—and Sylvia knew most of them too, believe it or not—as well as music with text, a person can create within their own imagination and their emotion, and their heart will be touched to appreciate this type of music. So I think it is vitally important that it should be included in the educational curriculum in the elementary schools up through the high schools. And I think that if we can get young people to attend these concerts, they need to be motivated and inspired by performers such as myself or people within a community who make sure these young people go to the New York Philharmonic Orchestra, go to the Metropolitan Opera. Sure, I'm not going to tell them to start out with Wagner, the Ring cycle, but go to the Magic Flute, go to the Marriage of Figaro, go and

Giuseppe Verdi

listen to Tchaikovsky's music where there is ballet dancing. I guarantee you that most of the children will love this music; it is very important in the development of their personalities, their hearts, their souls, and their minds.

Yen: And practice as well, and be uplifted. Can you perhaps say something to our audience of young people and their parents and teachers about the importance of this concert we are going to have at Carnegie Hall for Sylvia?

Estes: Yes. I'd like the young people to know that music knows no color; it has no boundaries. It is a gift that God has given people whether they are composers or singers or instrumentalists; let the young people know that by coming to this concert, you are going to hear some diversified neat classical music: the spirituals are going to be included, which is a different part of American culture and history, as well as composers such as Giuseppe Verdi, or Mozart, or other composers. Let them realize that they too can perform or sing that music, whether it be with the human voice or other instruments.

Yen: Thank You sir!
Estes: Thank you, and I wish your Foundation great success!

Yen: We look forward to seeing you in June!
Estes: Thank you, thank you!

Sylvia Olden Lee's Mission—and Ours

by Dennis Speed

June 13—When the Sylvia Olden Lee Centennial Chorus performs at Carnegie Hall this June 29, as part of the "Tribute to Sylvia Olden Lee, Master Musician and Teacher," sponsored by the Foundation for the Revival of Classical Culture, a promise to the Schiller Institute's late Cultural Advisory Board member (1917-2004) will be not merely kept, but renewed. Specifically, the Schiller Institute New York City Chorus—which has joined with the Convent Avenue Baptist Church Sanctuary Choir and other choruses and singers for this occasion—intends to establish a citywide choir of 1000-1500 people by the end of this year. This is a cultural "Apollo Project," launched in the spirit of that initiated by President John F. Kennedy, who was also born in 1917. It was proposed by Lyndon LaRouche during one, and later several of his Saturday Manhattan dialogues, and was finally adopted. Since that time the Schiller Institute New York City Chorus has grown from a handful of persons to 125-plus people. Two hundred twenty singers will take the stage at Carnegie, in addition to the seasoned professionals, colleagues, and collaborators of Sylvia who will pay their respects in the way that only great artists can do— bringing the works of genius to audible life, giving many people, particularly youth, access to them for the first time.

Sylvia Olden Lee taught and believed that the great prospective singers of the Classical stage were in the gas stations, waiting on tables in restaurants, parking cars, and flipping burgers throughout the post-industrial wasteland of America. They were not necessarily anywhere near the conservatories. Sylvia, who was not only meticulously trained, but who could recall and play from memory well over a thousand musical vocal pieces from opera, lieder, chanson, and oratorio, deeply believed in thorough musical preparation—so she was not opposing conservatory training. She

Schiller Institute

Sylvia Olden Lee, speaking at a Schiller Institute music seminar at Rankin Memorial Chapel at Howard University, in Washington, D.C. on Feb. 7, 1998, at the time of the visit from Germany of the Thomanerchor boys' choir to Washington.

simply noted, largely as a result of the work of her father, he of the famous Fisk Quartet, and of her own observations, that the proliferation of musical instruction, and the weekly practice of singing, if energetically spread throughout a community, resulted in the production of many more "voices of distinction" than might be assumed.

Members of the Schiller Institute, working with Sylvia's colleagues, including those who were and are great professional singers in their own right, have set out to demonstrate—using New York City as the laboratory—that Sylvia was right. The additional interesting feature of this, is that more languages are spoken in New York City than any other city in the world—perhaps as many as 800. Of these, 176 are spoken in the city's school system. New York City is therefore the natural "proving ground" for Sylvia's project, named after her mother, to "Save Young Lyric Voices In Advance."

Sylvia Olden Lee working with friends at the Sept. 1, 2001 ICLC/Schiller Institute Conference in Reston, Virginia. From left to right: William Warfield, Dorceal Duckens, and Dennis Speed.

Schiller Institute

Revolutionizing the Potential of Youth

How can you create a chorus out of people that all speak different languages, as in the Biblical story of the Tower of Babel, to sing as a single voice? That is no different from the idea of Alexander Hamilton's American Presidency. A singular voice of multiple states, a union that is *"e pluribus, unum."* Music, itself a language, hovers above these specific spoken (and sung) languages. In choral singing, in multiple parts, Bach's method of composition allows for every human voice-type to be placed, to be heard, and even to be featured, as all the other voices are simultaneously singing, as well. Rather than cacophony, an ever-richer harmony and counterposition of ideas was developed through the method of what is properly termed Classical polyphony. The basis, however, for the response in the human mind to that polyphony as a single idea, is that each mind is sovereign, and can therefore contain that polyphony, using it for its own form of individual expression through properly placing his or her voice within that polyphony.

For this, great teachers, and great music, are needed. But this is also the basis for revolutions in thought and changes in ideas that can be very quickly assimilated and transmitted from one individual and group to another. If such is successfully done, no population so educated can ever become petty and enslaved again. No such population so educated would ever tolerate what has happened to the United States since the two events

of September 11, 2001, and more profoundly, November 22, 1963.

Our educational institutions are the greatest expression of the failure of the political discourse and culture of the United States in the aftermath of Kennedy's assassination. Our physical economy could not have been so far degenerated had not the popular culture of the past 125 years degraded the mind of the citizen to such depths. Those who are six and seven years of age, as well as younger and older, are clearly not to blame. Liberating them from their imposed condition cannot be done by calling for the hanging of their teachers— who are themselves the product of the same system.

Classical music's method allows a powerful, if apparently indirect access to this deeper quality of thought in nearly all students; when Classical music doesn't work, there are always extra-musical reasons for that failure. Reversing the path of suicide in the United States requires that people be educated—"led out of"—their present self-imposed dark age. That requires getting past the policemen of consciousness, including the specific ideologies that plague particular national groups. This requires an epistemology which is generally unavailable at this time in trans-Atlantic school systems generally, and in the United States in particular. Only musical studies are generally capable of bringing this therapeutic corrective to the attention and the minds of the elementary school- and junior high school-aged child. Before they become the source of a descent into yet another, lower level of Hell, we have to "save these young lyric voices in advance," else, they will have no voice in any field.

It is this task to which the efforts of the Schiller Institute, including its participation in the Foundation for the Revival of Classical Culture's event, are directed.

About Sylvia Olden Lee

Excerpted from a 2004 article by Dennis Speed, which first appeared in the June 28, 2004 issue of the New Federalist *newspaper.*

Sylvia Olden Lee's father was a minister. "Daddy was born in 1884 and was the youngest of four children. Like Mama, Daddy had to work his way through Fisk, where he arrived in 1906. Part of Daddy's scholarship was to serve as a waiter, as well as to lead the singing in Sunday morning chapel. Many times they had visiting ministers. . . . Nobody knew what [they were] going to say. When the minister sat down after speaking, it was Daddy's job to break out *a cappella* in the choir with the very first thing that came into his head from the sermon, like, 'I never been to Heaven, but I been told. . . .' Then the whole church would join in unaccompanied: 'I know the Lord's laid His hands on me. Oh the gates are of pearl and the streets are gold . . .' It was a kind of *a cappella* Negro Spiritual. There weren't more than ten musicians in the congregation, but everybody sang four-part harmony. 'He sees all you do,' Daddy'd sing,

and they'd respond, 'He hears all you say . . .' Every Sunday a different one!"

Divorced from its setting in the church, the Spiritual is as impossible to understand, as it is impossible to understand Bach's *St. Matthew Passion* as a "concert performance piece." And *"Jauchzet Gott"* requires the same conviction, and spontaneous joy, as Sylvia's father had to glean, as an antiphonal counterpoint, from the Sunday sermon.

Her Family History

Sylvia's paternal grandfather was a slave who ran away from the Oldham plantation in Kentucky to fight with the Union Army at the beginning of the war. Her great-grandfather, Nelson Merry, was the founder of what was called the First Colored Baptist Church in Nashville, in 1853. He was also a slave, born in 1824,

---

'SCHILLER'S MUSIC TEACHER'

Sylvia Olden Lee and the German *Lied*

by Dennis Speed

June 13—The German *Lied* is the *Rosetta Stone* of Classical music. The project—initiated by Ludwig van Beethoven, and advanced and perfected by Franz Schubert, Robert Schumann, and Johannes Brahms, to spread, through these songs, the highest expression of Classical artistic principles of composition to the widest possible audience—was not limited to the German language, as Beethoven's settings of Irish, Scottish, and Welsh songs, as well as the Robert Burns settings done by several German and other composers, attest. It is, however, in the German *Lied*, that the Song achieved its highest expression.

Sylvia Lee was a master of the art of *Lieder* performance. It was her extraordinary integrity as a musician, that led her to achieve this level of perfection. Her studies with Gerhard Hüsch in Germany were essential for this. Hüsch recognized that Sylvia could understand what many miss—the Classical composers' appreciation of what America's Edgar Allan Poe once termed "The Power of Words." "When teaching

German *Lieder*, Gerhard Hüsch insisted that his students speak the lyrics as dramatic monologues before singing them, Sylvia told author Elizabeth Nash.

These *Lieder*, properly performed, embody the principle of Classical Theater. Tragedy is often their subject, but Tragedy viewed from the standpoint of the Sublime. Brahms' *"Immer leiser wird mein Schlummer,"* a song that Sylvia and singer Elvira Green often performed for Schiller Institute programs in Europe and America in 1994, perfectly illustrates the Idea of the Sublime, without flinching from a wrenching portrayal of the Tragic. Many often quote John Keats' famous "Ode On a Grecian Urn" that "Beauty is Truth, Truth Beauty," but how do we reconcile that with the Tragic? That demands artistry. That was the successful mission of the life of the Artist, Sylvia Olden Lee.

Since the 1873 and 1877 visits of the Fisk Jubilee Singers to Europe, there has been a trans-Atlantic discussion process among Classical artists, including Brahms and Dvorak, with American musicians, and particularly many musicians of African heritage, on the identity of the Idea of the Sublime, embodied in the German *Lied* and the Negro Spiritual. Contrary to the unfortunate commentaries written by those who have failed to comprehend the Classical composers' devotion to the Poetic Principle, this is not a "multi-cultural issue." If one listens, for example, to contralto Marian

---

and freed in 1845, after being taught to read, against the law, by the pastor of the First Baptist Church. (The First Colored Baptist Church was the segregated spin-off of the original church to which he was passed on, as property, by the wife of his former master, upon her death in 1840.)

Nelson Merry got to Nashville as a result of the refusal of his Indian mother, Sylvia's paternal great-great-grandmother—refusing to continue to walk to Oklahoma in Andrew Jackson's and Martin van Buren's genocidal "Trail of Tears," the attempted extermination, through deportation, of the Cherokee Nation of North and South Carolina, Georgia, Alabama, and Mississippi. Because she refused to walk any further, the children, including Sylvia's great-grandfather, were sold to various masters. Sylvia's grandfather, father, and mother were also students at Fisk College, founded by members of the American Missionary Association to provide the basis for a Classical education to former slaves, in 1866.

The Fisk University education was emphatically not to "educate the newly freed slaves to their expected station." It was not "post-slavery skills 101." In the music curriculum at Fisk, for example, it was noted by this author, in 1994, that the section of the curriculum which discussed prerequisites for competence in piano, emphasized the students' study of Bach's "two-voiced and three-voiced inventions," not today's musically illiterate "two and three-part inventions." Students were offered, and encouraged to study, Greek, Hebrew, and Latin, often in relation to religious study, but also for basic literacy.

Anderson and pianist Franz Rupp perform Schumann's *"Stille Tränen"* followed by the Spiritual, "Crucifixion," the identity of intention that imbues the spirit of the two performances is audible. It cannot be so, not if the performances are truthful, unless the substance of the message behind the words, is also identical. It was George Shirley, William Warfield, Sylvia Lee, and Robert McFerrin, who insisted, on the behalf of Musical Truth, that this identity in Intention, of both the *Lied*, and the Spiritual, be the standard of performance, in their 1990s performances and teaching with the Schiller Institute.

Dvorak spoke of the same identity of Classical intention to his friend, musician Harry Burleigh, who introduced Dvorak to the Spirituals, by singing them to him for hours at a time. Dvorak exclaimed to Burleigh, that he heard the same Idea behind the Spirituals, as he heard behind Beethoven's great symphonic themes. Roland Hayes proved this to initially hostile, and then adoring, German audiences in 1927, much to the chagrin of certain of his American counterparts, who were a bit surprised when the now-converted German audience members exclaimed, "At last! An American who can actually sing our songs!" Hayes recognized what Sylvia Lee practiced all the time, and what Gerhard Hüsch must have appreciated about her from their first meeting. They were not only "the songs of the Germans," although they were also the songs of the Germans. These were, like the Spirituals, songs of, and for, all people everywhere.

Of course, therefore, Sylvia and the Schiller Institute would have to meet. Of course, she would find herself a closer and closer interlocutor with Lyndon LaRouche and Helga LaRouche, whose love of the German *Lied* mirrors their love of humanity, as Sylvia's love of humanity mirrors her love of music. The present tense is appropriate here, for the Artist never dies. All Nature sings the song of the Artist, always; for the Artist, as Schiller taught us, is he who stands at the shoulders of God in his Creation, for whom all things are new, and all things renewed, forever.

> *Über mein Bett erhebt sich ein Baum,*
> *Drin singt die junge Nachtigall;*
> *Sie singt von lauter Liebe,*
> *Ich hör es sogar im Traum.*

> Over my bed, there rises a tree;
> In it the young nightingale sings;
> It sings of nothing but love, of nothing but love;
> I hear it, I hear it even in my dreams, even in my dreams.

So may we all, hear Sylvia, even in our dreams, of a better world, that will be of her, and the Artist's, making.

The Fisk Jubilee Singers

Sylvia's Civil War-veteran grandfather had a sister, Elizabeth Merry, who also attended Fisk, and was part of the Fisk Jubilee Singers, the group that was responsible, more than any other, for making the African-American Spirituals known throughout the world. In two remarkable and exhaustive tours, they acquainted particularly Germany, Bohemia (the present-day Czech Republic, as well as Slovakia), and England, with these songs, not as a specialty, but as embedded in Classical repertoire programs, of which all the members of the ensemble were accomplished performers. The Spirituals would be, less than twenty years later, the basis for the attempt by Johannes Brahms and his associate, Antonin Dvorak, to create an American practice of Classical musical composition in the United States through Jeanette Thurber's National Conservatory of Music. Dvorak's devoted study of the Negro Spiritual, as conveyed to him by the singer, musician, and composer Harry Burleigh, won Dvorak the undying enmity of those in both Europe and America committed to the lie of "black cultural inferiority." Although aborted, echoes of Dvorak's and Brahms's efforts would persist up through their destruction by the Frankfurt School and the Congress for Cultural Freedom in the late 1940s and 1950s.

Sylvia's mother, a formidable pianist and vocalist, was offered the opportunity to sing at New York's Metropolitan Opera in 1912, but refused, when she was informed that she, who had blonde hair and blue eyes,

---

'Music is Hard Work!'

June 13—"I don't feel that my approach as a vocal coach of interpretation is unique. But I probably am unique in beating the devil out of singers to help them create an interpretation meant to be closest to the composer's intention for his opera, oratorio, *lied*, chanson, or song." Sylvia Olden Lee could demand and elicit a caliber of musical and intellectual excellence from singers that other teachers could not, because she demanded the same excellence from herself. Here is some of the advice she offered, as recorded by author Elizabeth Nash in her book, *The Memoirs of Sylvia Olden Lee, Premier African-American Classical Vocal Coach: Who is Sylvia*:

> Try setting your alarm at 6:15. Don't get out of bed. Don't go to the bathroom. Reach for your score and open it. Don't make a sound. Read it as you would a novel and put yourself in the place of the character. Try to acquire most of your artistic knowledge in quietness. It is your duty as a singer to know everything on the page except the printer's mark at the bottom.

> For an opera, singers should be familiar with the libretto and its source, whether it's Shakespeare or Johann Wolfgang von Goethe. It's not enough to know that Gounod wrote *Faust*. Who wrote the original story? They don't have to be authorities on the composer's and dramatic or literary author's lives. But they should at least know the author's intention and what prompted the composer to set this text to music.

> ... For a song, singers should know who wrote the poem. It must be superb, since the composer decided it was worthy of being set to music.... Initially, the singers should look up the poet's life and read one other of his works, so as to take on his mantle. Then they should sit and silently study their song's poem. Next, they should say it aloud to discover the rhythms and words to be accented. If you take the tune away, some singers can't do the song. That's why I insist: "learn the text first!" Mr. Rudolf stated: "Both Beethoven and Verdi, never having written literary texts in their lives, said on their death beds: Pay attention to the words." They really could have said: "Pay attention to the thoughts."

> ... Singers can hold their scores if they must, but there's got to be some interpretation there! When teaching German *lieder*, Gerhard Hüsch insisted that his students speak the lyrics as dramatic monologues before singing them....

> ... But no one can put the meaning in your head. You have to bring it out of yourself!

Opera Buff/Baroque Duet 1992 Documentary

Sylvia Olden Lee and Kathleen Battle in a working session in 1992.

Schiller Institute.

Sylvia Olden Lee speaking at a Feb. 18-21, 1994 Schiller Institute conference in Washington, D.C.

would be expected to "pass for white"—to deny that she was of African-American ethnic origin. Her father, a member of the legendary Fisk Quartet, which also included the extraordinary singer Roland Hayes (1887-1977), became a minister and civil rights organizer, who was run out of Alabama by the Ku Klux Klan when Sylvia was a young child, in the 1920s. He later successfully forced the first performance by an African-American conductor, heading a Classical orchestra, below the Mason-Dixon line, in 1953. The conductor was Everett Lee, Sylvia's husband and a master violinist.

Sylvia was to force the Metropolitan Opera to allow accomplished musicians of African-American origin through its doors, by first becoming a vocal coach at the Met, and then suggesting to her colleague Max Rudolf that an American of African descent, Carol Brice, sing the role of Ulrica in Giuseppe Verdi's *Un Ballo in Maschera*. It was Marian Anderson who actually performed that role that year, which opened the American Classical stage to all those who had been forced away from this field from the time that Dvorak had been driven out of the United States, in 1895. This was followed by the great Robert McFerrin singing at the Met that same year. Sylvia became, through the years, the premier consultant for literally hundreds of singers, and had, as of

EIRNS/Stuart Lewis

Sylvia Olden Lee, speaking at a May 28, 1994 National Music Conference in Washington, D.C., entitled "For a Marian Anderson National Conservatory of Music Movement." It was held at Rankin Chapel at Howard University.

1993, become more familiar as "Kathleen Battle's teacher."

With the Schiller Institute

The Schiller Institute worked with Sylvia Lee for just over ten years. Her pedagogical method was instantly identified as identical with that of the best of humanist thinkers and teachers. It was witheringly honest, often hilarious, and always focused on the essentials. In the last years, she most loved working with the LaRouche Youth Movement, which she had the opportunity to do on the West Coast and in Philadelphia. She was not merely in agreement with LaRouche on "cultural matters"; she was a financial contributor to the LaRouche Presidential campaign, and actively supported it whenever she could.

II. Humanity Starts on a New Path

Russia, China Develop the Arctic—Will the United States Join?

by Mike Billington

June 12—Russia and China are escalating their efforts to develop one of the last, relatively untouched frontiers for mankind on Earth—the vast expanse of the Arctic's rich resource base. While Russia's huge coastline on the Arctic Ocean is the primary base of operations, China is heavily engaged in building the infrastructure needed to make the exploitation of these resources feasible.

Will the U.S. under President Trump engage in this process? The answer to this question will play a crucial role in the broader issue that will, to a significant degree, determine the fate of mankind—whether or not Trump will fully integrate the United States into the Belt and Road Initiative, the New Silk Road process first promoted by Lyndon and Helga LaRouche in the 1990s, and now fully adopted and implemented by Chinese President Xi Jinping on behalf of all nations on Earth.

A major physical driver for this initiative is the fact that the northeast passage—the route from Asia to Europe via the Arctic Ocean—has become increasingly viable due to the receding of the Arctic ice cap. While the green movement is quick to claim that (non-existent) manmade climate change is responsible for this recession of the Arctic ice cap, the Russian government and Russian scientists (among others) have proven that this is a cyclical phenomenon unrelated to carbon—and indeed, very beneficial to mankind. Not only is trade facilitated by this reces-sion, but Arctic resources are also rendered more accessible — if the world chooses to take advantage of the new circumstances.

One Belt, One Road, One Circle

Hu Angang, a leading Chinese economist at Tsinghua University, coined the term "One Circle"—referring to the encirclement of the entire Eurasian land

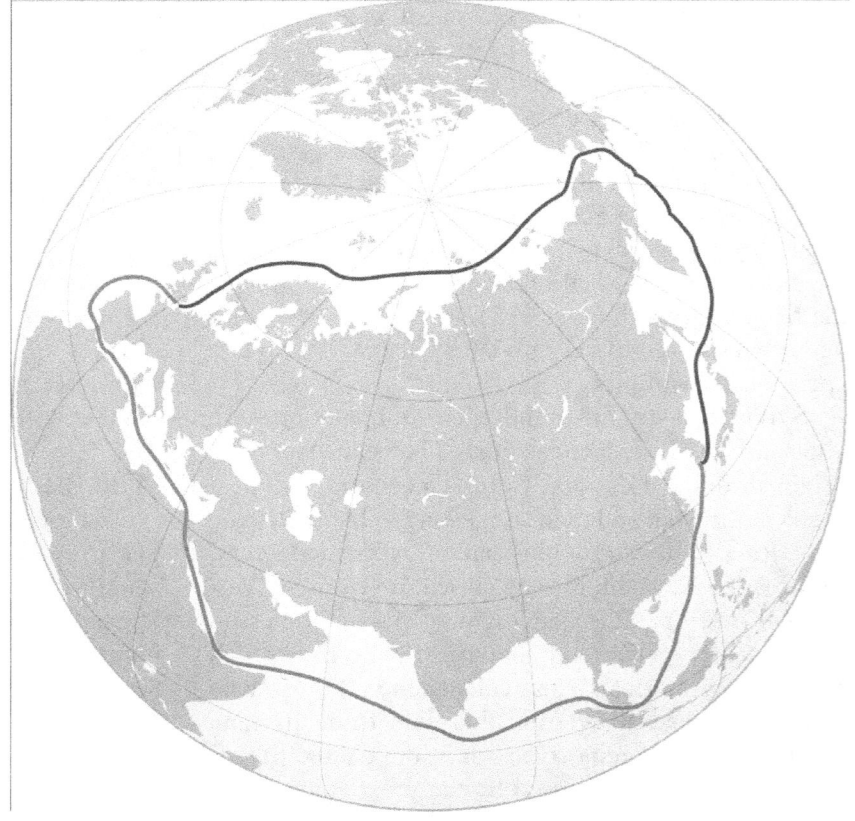

Kazakhstan

A graphical comparison between the Northern Sea Route (blue) and the southern maritime route (red).

mass by the completion of the northeast passage—to go along with the "One Belt, One Road" policy initiated by President Xi Jinping in 2013. The New Silk Road Economic Belt, connecting Asia, Europe, and Africa over land, and the 21st Century Maritime Silk Road, connecting Eurasia, Africa, and the Americas by sea, can now be joined by the Arctic "One Circle" route, cutting shipping time by over 30% from East Asia to Europe.

Beside shipping time, the resources waiting to be developed—waiting only for the human race to develop the technologies needed to facilitate such development in a harsh environment, in a manner acceptable to human habitation—include vast

DSME

South Korean shipbuilder Daewoo Shipbuilding Marine Engineering (DSME) completed the construction of the first Arctic LNG carrier, the Christophe de Margerie.

deposits of gold and other minerals, as well as an estimated 30% of the world's undiscovered natural gas and 13% of undiscovered oil, according to the U.S. Geological Survey.

While issues of sovereignty apply to the resources near the borders of the Arctic nations (Russia, United States, Norway, Finland, Sweden, and Denmark), the vast territory of the Arctic is mostly outside of territorial waters, and is thus subject only to the United Nations Convention on the Law of the Sea (UNCLOS), which allows only for joint development of the resources under consensus agreements. Governing this process is the Arctic Council, comprising the six Arctic nations, with others present as observers, including China. China considers itself a "near-Arctic" state, and points out that the region holds "the inherited wealth of all humankind." The last biennial summit of the Arctic Council took place in Juneau, Alaska in March, where Finland took over as president for the current two-year term.

On his way to visit President Trump in Florida in April, President Xi Jinping stopped in Finland to discuss Finland's role in the Belt and Road, but he also arranged for Finland to represent China in meetings of the Arctic Council.

While the deliberations of the Council have thus far avoided efforts to introduce geopolitical conflicts, some members of U.S. Congress have used the fact that

Russia has security concerns along its extensive Arctic border, to call on the United States to prepare military capacities to challenge Russian dominance of the region. That is absurd, given that the United States has a grand total of one functioning ice-breaker, while Russia has 40, and is in the process of building or ordering (primarily from South Korea) the construction of dozens more.

Just this week, President Putin oversaw the christening and naming of the world's largest liquefied natural gas (LNG) ice-breaker in St. Petersburg, built for Russia by South Korea's Daewoo Shipbuilding and Marine Engineering Corporation. Clearly not intended for military purposes, the ship will be used at the Yamal project on the Yamal Peninsula on the Arctic, at the northern end of the Ural Mountains. This region holds huge natural gas deposits that are being developed by a consortium involving Russia's Novatek, France's Total, and the China National Petroleum Corporation. The ship is the most modern tanker of a high-ice class, and will become the flagship in a fleet of 15 similar vessels. The Yamal project aims to produce 16.5 million tons of LNG a year.

Speaking at the christening, Putin said: "The Yamal project paved the way for the Arctic route. It will contribute to the development of the energy industry in the whole world, as well as Russia and Europe.... Yamal LNG plays an important role in the development of the

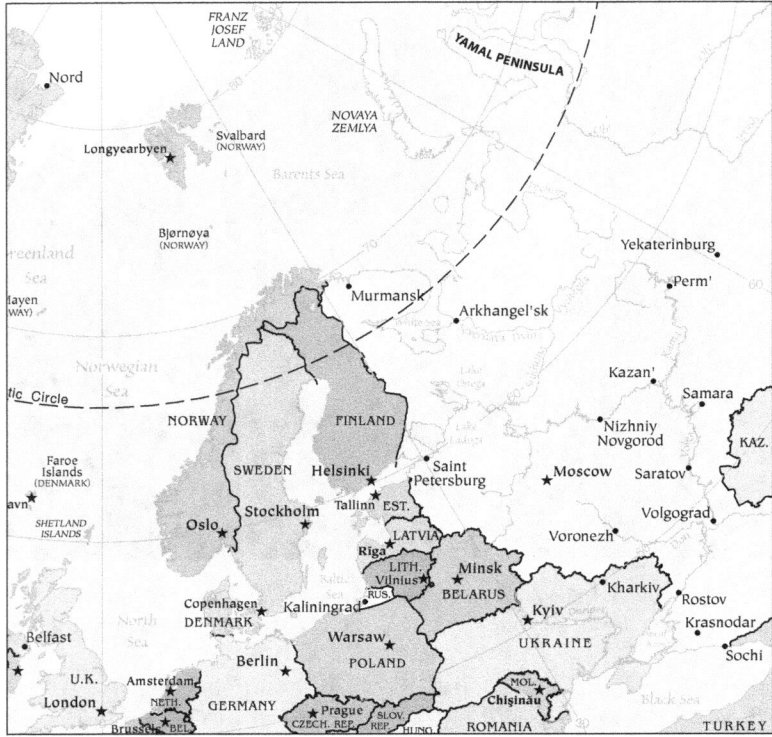

Russia is building a Northern Latitude Railway to connect the Yamal Peninsula within the Arctic Circle (dashed circle) to the region of the Ural Mountains to the south (mountains not shown). China's Poly Group is planning a deep water port and a southward rail connection in the Arkhangelsk region, just south of the Arctic Circle.

A long-range intention of the Russian development of Arctic facilities is the testing of structures required for human outposts on the Moon and on Mars.

U.S. Cooperation

A ministerial meeting of the Arctic Council in Fairbanks, Alaska on May 11 was projected to be contentious by those who are trying to sabotage President Trump's effort to establish cooperative and friendly relations with Russia. Such projections were proven futile. Among the outcomes of the meeting, chaired by the United States, was the signing of a binding agreement to facilitate cooperation in scientific research in the region, ensuring that scientists and their equipment and data can flow more freely across international borders within the Arctic. An Arctic Shipping Traffic Database has been set up, while a new Arctic Economic Council and a Task Force on Improved Connectivity are becoming operational.

David Balton, the U.S. Deputy Assistant Secretary of State for Oceans and Fisheries, who represented the U.S. at the meeting, countered the neocon dreams of confrontation with Russia, saying that the Arctic remains stable and peaceful. "Through the Arctic Council, we have a venue that has been doing very well in promoting international cooperation among all eight nations, including Russia," Balton said, adding that "Whatever other differences may exist between the United States, Russia, and other members of the Arctic Council, and Russia related to other parts of the world, don't manifest themselves in the world of the Arctic Council. That has remained a very cooperative body."

The Wilson Center's Arctic Circle Forum is hosting a conference in Washington on June 21-22, titled "The United States and Russia in the Arctic." Balton will speak, along with many others from the United States, Russia, and other Arctic Council nations. It is precisely this kind of cooperation—pushing forward the frontiers of development and the frontiers of human knowledge—that, like the New Silk Road, is moving the world into a new paradigm of peace through development.

Northern Sea Route, and in the further study and exploration of the Arctic. I am counting on the successful launch of new, promising, large-scale projects with our French, Chinese, and foreign partners, as well as on our growing cooperation in the extremely rich Arctic Region."

Russia is also building a Northern Latitude Railway to connect Yamal with the Ural regions to the south and the nation's transportation arteries, ensuring year-round transport of the region's mineral resources.

In another major development zone, that of the Arkhangelsk region south of Murmansk near the Norway and Finland border, China's Poly Group Corporation is planning a $5.5 billion development project, involving a new deep water port and a rail connection to the south. The intention is to ship coal, fertilizer, oil, and other goods from Siberia and the Urals via the Arctic, and then south by rail. Igor Orlov, the governor of Arkhangelsk, estimates that the project will generate 40,000 jobs when it is completed in 2023.

NASA Presents New Astronaut Class at Johnson Space Center

by Kesha Rogers

June 7—NASA introduced twelve new astronauts today at the Johnson Space Center in Houston, Texas. This was a record year in the history of NASA: The twelve astronauts, five of whom are women, were selected out of a candidate pool of over 18,000 applicants, more applicants than ever before. The astronauts will begin training for missions into Earth orbit and deep space. The astronaut class of 2017 was the 22nd class of American space flight trainees since 1959.

I attended this very inspiring event, reporting for *21st Century Science & Technology*. There to bring greetings from Washington on behalf of President Donald Trump and the White House, was Vice President Mike Pence. The Vice President joined NASA leaders—including acting administrator Robert Lightfoot and director of Houston flight operations Brian Kelly—in announcing the new astronauts. Several elected officials attended, including Senator Ted Cruz, Congressman Lamar Smith, Congressman Jim Bridenstine, and Texas Governor Greg Abbott. Many other local officials and others representing congressional offices were also present. The presentation of the as-tronauts took place inside Johnson Space Center's Space Vehicle Mockup Facility, in front of a full-scale engineering model of NASA's Orion spacecraft.

The full text of the Vice President's speech can be found at NASA.gov. He said in part,

> To the members of this new class of American astronauts, I say congratulations. ... As American astronauts, you may yet return our nation to the Moon. You may be the first to travel to Mars. You may have experiences that we can only imagine.

Vice President Pence made a promise that—

> NASA will have the resources and support you need to continue to make history, to push the boundary of human knowledge, and to advance American leadership to the boundless frontier of space.
>
> Under President Donald Trump, America will lead in space once again, and the world will follow.

NASA/Robert Markowitz

The 2017 NASA Astronaut Class.

Pence referenced President Trump's relaunching of a National Space Council after more than two decades, which the Vice President will chair. Pence said, "America needs a national space council once again," and explained that—

Twice before in our nation's history, our nation has had a federal body charged with advising the President on national policy and strategy for space. It was under the council's watch that America put the first man in outer space, and put a man on the Moon in less than a decade between. ... Our national space council will re-energize the pioneering spirit of America in Space. ... We must reorient our civilian space program toward deep space exploration, and provide the capabilities for America to maintain a constant presence in low Earth orbit and beyond.

He referred to increased collaboration with commercial space industry, stating,

The American spirit is as limitless as space itself, and by tapping the bottomless well of American innovation through increased collaboration with commercial space industries, we can seize opportunities that will benefit our nation and our people for generations to come.

Pence summoned the inspiration of President John F. Kennedy when he said,

I know the path you have chosen is hard. But as President John F. Kennedy said not far from here in 1962, we do not choose to do these things "because they are easy," but rather "because they are hard. ... because that challenge is one that we are willing to accept, one we are unwilling to postpone," and that challenge is "one which we intend to win."

Vice President Pence affirmed, "And we will win." He later continued,

Once again we reach out our hands to touch the heavens, and raise our heads to gaze with wonder at the stars—and the heroes that have courage to explore them. And you twelve will be part of our vanguard. You are true heroes—true patriots—and true trailblazers in the best American tradition.

Following the ceremony, I joined other members of the media for one-on-one discussion with NASA representatives speaking on behalf of NASA's Commercial Crew Program, Orion spacecraft, and the International Space Station (ISS). There was also a Q&A session with the astronauts. Some very exciting discoveries are being made in deep space exploration, and with ISS.

The Necessary Economic Platform

There is still no mention of a choice for NASA administrator, and the emphasis on commercial space flight as a means of cutting corners and saving money, shows how desperately we require a national space mission and the vision that inspired the nation and the world under President John F. Kennedy.

This is a moment in our nation's history in which Americans should be very proud of the great potential being unleashed. But we have to harness that potential. We will only achieve our goal of returning America to greatness in space through increased international cooperation, including collaborating with China, as well as with our other international partners.

We must revive our national mission in space exploration—one that will contribute to the economic progress of our nation and all nations around the world, while providing the highest level of responsibility for the safety and the lives of our astronauts, as they venture out to make new discoveries.

The first step toward the implementation of our national mission in space is an economic recovery program for the United States that will immediately implement Lyndon LaRouche's Four Laws, starting with the reinstatement of Glass-Steagall, followed by the implementation of a National Credit system. We need immediate investment in a national infrastructure platform, including a space platform for the development of new technologies and new resources, that will advance the whole of human knowledge, and allow us to increase the standard of living of every person on Earth. There can be no shortcuts to achieving our national goal of restoring America's leadership in space. We can no longer allow failure as an option in our commitment to space.

As a NASA representative working on the ISS stated, "No single nation is going to go on an exploration mission by itself. We are going to go as a species."

Every Day Counts In Today's Showdown To Save Civilization

That's why you need EIR's **Daily Alert Service**, a strategic overview compiled with the input of Lyndon LaRouche, and delivered to your email 5 days a week.

The election of Donald Trump to the Presidency of the Untied States has launched a new global era whose character has yet to be determined. The Obama-Clinton drive toward confrontation with Russia has been disrupted--but what will come next?

Over the next weeks and months there will be a pitched battle to determine the course of the Trump Administration. Will it pursue policies of cooperation with Russia and China in the New Silk Road, as the President-Elect has given some signs of? Will it follow through against Wall Street with Glass-Steagall?

The opposition to these policies will be fierce. If there is to be a positive outcome to this battle, an informed citizenry must do its part--intervening, educating, inspiring. That's why you need the EIR Daily Alert more than ever.

TUESDAY, NOVEMBER 22, 2016

Volume 3, Number 65

EIR Daily Alert Service

P.O. Box 17390, Washington, DC 20041-0390

- Only Global Solutions, Based on New Principles, Can Work
- Tulsi Gabbard Meets with Donald Trump Regarding Syria
- Robert Kagan Throws in the Towel, Complains U.S. Is Becoming 'Solipsistic'
- War Party Moving To Preempt Trump-Putin Reset
- Syrian Army Makes More Progress in Aleppo
- Duterte Gives OK to Nuclear Power for Philippines
- Europe Will Suffer from Maintaining Russia Sanctions
- Former Chilean Diplomat Confirmed, 'We Will Joyfully Welcome Xi Jinping'
- Duterte and Putin Establish Philippines-Russia Cooperation
- François Fillon, Pro-Russian Thatcherite, Wins First Round of French Right-Wing Presidential Primary

EDITORIAL

Only Global Solutions, Based on New Principles, Can Work

The British and Obama Never Gave Up on Rigging Our Election: Let's Stop Their Coup Now!

by Barbara Boyd

June 11—After viewing fired FBI Director James Comey's testimony on June 8, Lyndon LaRouche called upon the American people to immediately shut down the coup underway against President Trump. LaRouche said, "This is an FBI type operation to destroy the United States, and, if it is not stopped, the world will face general warfare."

On June 7, former Director of National Intelligence (DNI) James Clapper openly touted the *real reason* for the coup against Trump in an unhinged speech in Australia, granting full leave to his inner swine: Clapper

declared that Trump's unforgivable sin is the President's openness to collaborating with Putin and Russia and his refusal to back down on his campaign promise to end the Bush/Obama policy of perpetual wars, a key reason why he was elected.

Clapper ranted that it is in Putin's and Russia's "genes" to attack the United States. Since Trump has pursued better relations and shared intelligence with Russia on terrorism, Clapper raved, Watergate [where Richard Nixon committed proven crimes] paled in comparison to Russiagate [where both Clapper and

Courtesy Senate Select Committee on Intelligence

Director of National Intelligence James Clapper (center) testifies before the Senate Select Committee on Intelligence Feb. 9. Clapper was accompanied by FBI Director James Comey (left), CIA Director John Brennan (right) and other top intelligence and security officials.

Comey have testified to date that the President has committed no crimes]. Clapper also told the Aussies to target China, accusing the Chinese, without any offer of proof, of meddling in Australia's elections. Comey backed Clapper in his testimony on June 8, attempting to wax eloquent in response to Senator Joe Manchin, about how Putin exists with one purpose in mind: to shred and dismember the United States.

In fact, according to James Comey's testimony, the President has not even been under FBI investigation, despite months of frantic and breathless media and congressional claims to the contrary. As we shall see here, the only actual crimes that have thus far been committed are those of Obama and his holdovers in the intelligence community who launched a coup against the President, at the behest of the British, based on Trump's rejection of the British foreign policy to isolate and militarily encircle Russia and China, prevent the emergence of China's new paradigm for global economic development, and maintain the status of the Anglo-American imperialists as the world's sole hegemon, even if it means nuclear war. Hillary Clinton and Barack Obama had sworn allegiance to this London/ Wall Street creed; Trump dumped all over it.

According to the "narrative" provided by the media to the American population, around June 2016, two weeks after Donald Trump was declared the Republican nominee, the Democratic National Committee (DNC) discovered that its computers had been "hacked." It immediately called in a private company, CrowdStrike, which declared the source of the attacks to be Russian, particularly *Russian state entities*.

On July 22, shortly before the Democratic Party convention, Wikileaks published internal Democratic National Committee documents, which showed that the DNC was openly conspiring to destroy the candidacy of Clinton's rival, Bernie Sanders. Barack Obama's DNC Chairman, Debbie Wasserman Shultz, was forced to resign over the ensuing scandal, along with other DNC employees.

In October, Wikileaks published emails from John Podesta, Hillary Clinton's campaign manager and the leader of the Center for American Progress, the "idea" factory for the Obama Administration. The Podesta emails elaborated on Hillary Clinton's fawning Wall Street speeches and the scummier financial dealings of the Clinton Foundation. They also showed that Donna

White House
Barack Obama and Hillary Clinton at an Obama-Clinton rally in Orlando, Florida on Oct. 20, 2008.

Brazile, a commentator for CNN and the then Vice-Chair of the Democratic Party, helped Hillary cheat in the CNN sponsored Presidential debates, by feeding her official debate questions beforehand.

Before proceeding to the whodunit part of our presentation, it is urgent to remind you that everything exposed by Wikileaks was truthful; the events exposed actually did happen.

In an obvious attempt to deflect from the damaging proof that Obama and Clinton were, in fact, rigging the election, and had functioned as the corrupt tools of Wall Street and the British, the Clinton campaign played the "Putin demon" black propaganda card. This was hardly a new gambit for either Obama or Clinton. Their dangerous propaganda campaign for war with Russia was already in high gear when the Wikileaks documents appeared. Most informed observers believe that if Hillary Clinton were elected, she would have immediately acted upon her bellicose rhetoric, putting the entire human race at risk in the process. Typical is the *Washington Post* signal opinion piece by the National Endowment for Democracy's Carl Gershman in October 2016, calling upon the establishment to "summon the will" to overthrow Putin.[1] This war drive began following Obama's coups in Libya and Ukraine, and Putin's responsive interventions in Crimea and Syria.[2]

---

1. Gershman similarly signaled the impending coup in Ukraine, identifying it as the National Endowment for Democracy's "biggest prize," in a *Washington Post* article of September 26, 2013.

2. One of the more amazing ironies of post World War II history finds so-called liberal Democrats, led by Barack Obama and Hillary Clinton,

I. Organizing To Overthrow the U.S. Presidency: the Police Blotter

There are several anomalies lurking beneath the surface in the media's official "narrative" about the alleged Russian hack attack.

1. It has never been established that whatever happened inside computers at the DNC or to John Podesta's gmail account had anything to do with the damning Wikileaks releases. Wikileaks has insisted that the releases are internal leaks, not hacks. No less than one Barack Obama has stated that this is a major hole in the "Putin did it" evidentiary scenario.

2. CrowdStrike is run by a violently anti-Putin Russian émigré, the Atlantic Council's Dmitri Alperovitch, and one George Kurtz. Kurtz is a personal computer security veteran who founded CrowdStrike as a special project of the longstanding Anglo-American investment entity known as Warburg Pincus. CrowdStrike has multiple security contracts with U.S. and foreign intelligence agencies. The FBI never examined the hacked computers, nor did anyone else in the intelligence community. Rather, they relied on forensics provided by CrowdStrike. Alperovitch alleged, shortly thereafter, that the same hacking gear used by the Russians to hack the DNC had also been used by the Russians to hack various guidance systems of Ukrainian government missiles in Ukraine, a claim that was instantaneously debunked by almost the entire international computer security community.

3. One of the alleged internal alarms at the DNC that there was something wrong with their computers, was the April 2016 report of staffer and consultant Alexandra Chalupa that her computer had been hacked. She was allegedly investigating the ties of then Trump campaign chairman Paul Manafort to Russia and Putin, working with "journalists" and intelligence officials in Ukraine to discredit Manafort and Trump. In other words, she was a Clinton opposition research consultant—in the vernacular, an "oppo" operative gathering intelligence against Hillary's rival for the presidency—working with *Ukrainian and other intelligence agencies*, who otherwise collaborate with MI6, the CIA, and with George Soros and the National Endowment for Democracy's Project Democracy apparatus. Chalupa, a violently anti-Putin Ukrainian-American was using a Yahoo email account to conduct her very sensitive covert espionage. Yahoo has been repeatedly hacked by alleged "state actors" of various sorts since 2014.

4. So, Clinton's "oppo" efforts, massively funded by her political action committees, involved collaboration, even at this point, with active or former Anglo-American intelligence agents and foreign nation states, one of which, Ukraine, was in a self-declared state of war with Putin's Russia. The allegations concerning Chalupa's computer were initially used to fuel the bogus media campaign against Manafort, who was then Trump's campaign chairman. Manafort's alleged "sin" was that he, like Tony Podesta, John Podesta's brother, did public relations work for Victor Yanukovych, the duly elected President of Ukraine, and also lobbied, legally, for some Russian clients. Subsequent media attacks on Manafort, based on never proven "illicit Russian ties," forced his resignation from Trump's campaign. As previously noted, Yanukovych was overthrown in 2014 by Obama, in an illegal color revolution coup which used armed neo-Nazis as violent "special forces," to overturn a free, fair, and EU-certified election.

5. The intelligence community initially didn't publicly buy into the Obama/Clinton "oppo" line about Russian interference in the elections and deep Trump ties to Russia. Clapper, for example, stated early on that he did not know "what all the hyperventilation is about." Clapper alluded to the fact that cyber-war is simply what state intelligence agencies do, the U.S. included. Clapper also knows that the U.S. has intervened to rig elections throughout the world, including Russia's elections, and was probably chary to open that door, absent significant preparation.[3] So, after their initial Putin demon gambit landed with a public thud and put, ironically, war and peace squarely on the public's agenda, Clinton and Obama produced yet more new leaks from anonymous sources. They claimed that election systems in Illinois and Arizona had been hacked by the Russians, and that the Russians were the source of major hacks at media organizations, including the *New York Times* and CNN. These fake stories appeared and

---

engaging, since their Ukraine coup, in a McCarthyite extravaganza targeting Russia and Putin, which rivals that of the infamous Roy Cohn and Senator Joseph McCarthy. Actually, this is not irony at all; the social democrats have simply dropped their pretenses. No longer are we seeing "fascism with a democratic face." We are seeing fascism.

---

3. Clapper looks like an imitation Yoda robot with extra-big ears. Recently he said, with respect to Trump and the Russians, that his "dashboard instrument warning lights were on." Where oh where are the great cartoonists of yesteryear?

disappeared from public view in short order.

6. In June 2016, however, at the same time that the DNC was first announcing that its computers had been hacked by the Russians, Christopher Steele, the former head of Britain's MI6 Russia desk, with very current connections to the highest level of the Queen's Secret Services, began producing the first of seventeen dossiers for the Clinton campaign's Russia smear operation against Trump. Steele had a longstanding prior relationship with James Comey's FBI, and had previously been paid for producing allegations against candidate Trump by Jeb Bush's

CC/Laurie Nevay-IMG

The MI6 Building at Vauxhall Cross, London. The building also houses the headquarters of the British Secret Intelligence Service (SIS).

supporters. According to press accounts, British Intelligence's Steele's reports, laundered through the Clinton campaign, were the basis for beginning the unprecedented FBI counterintelligence investigation of the Trump presidential campaign in July 2016. The British Steele reports were used by Comey's FBI as the road map for the FBI's investigation.

7. On July 5, 2016, Comey gave his now famous illicit press conference (in direct contravention of Justice Department rules and prosecutorial ethics regarding unindicted cases), closing the Hillary Clinton email investigation. Facts he disclosed in that press conference indicated that Clinton and/or her aides (who the Obama Justice Department immunized from prosecution) had not only abused classified material but had also obstructed justice, setting off an entirely predictable controversy in the midst of a presidential election. On July 10, 2016, Seth Rich, a DNC staffer involved in its computer operations and an avid supporter of Bernie Sanders, was murdered under suspicious circumstances near his home in Washington, D.C. Wikileaks has directly implied that Rich was one of its sources of the explosive DNC emails demonstrating that Clinton and Obama were rigging the election.

8. An FBI counterintelligence investigation, such as that directed at the Trump campaign, often involves secret FISA Court authorized surveillance which cannot be discussed under the law. The penalty is ten years in prison. These investigations can and often do also involve classified surveillance conducted pursuant to a different authority, Executive Order 12333. Intelligence officials are *authorized to directly lie* about even the existence of surveillance conducted pursuant to E.O. 12333, in order to protect "sources and methods."[4] According to media reports about the Trump investigation, the FBI first submitted a warrant request to the FISA Court that was so overly broad that it was rejected. It was an invitation for a fishing expedition. A narrowed request, which focused on Carter Page, was accepted by the court and renewed on various occasions. Page was a walk-in foreign policy "volunteer" to the Trump campaign who previously served as an FBI source in a Russian spy ring investigation conducted in New York City in 2013. He also has publicly stated that he reports all his activities with Russians to the FBI and CIA. His repeated offers to testify before the Congressional committees involved in Russiagate have been rebuffed.

9. There was plenty more actual evidence to suggest that candidate Trump's skepticism about Russian hacking was entirely warranted. Former NSA whistleblowers pointed out that if there was a Russian hack, the NSA would know about it, and immediately back the conclusion with evidence, *which it did not*. Wikileaks stated that its source for the documents was not Russia, but an insider, a whistle-blower. Former

---

4. It is probable that this is why James Clapper was not prosecuted for perjury when he lied to Congress that American citizens were not subject to mass surveillance four months before the Edward Snowden revelations of same. The bulk of the surveillance occurs under E.O. 12333.

Aerial view of the GCHQ in Cheltenham, Gloucestershire.

defenceimages.mod.uk

U.S. intelligence professionals, including the NSA's William Binney and the CIA's Ray McGovern, provided a detailed report supporting Wikileaks' whistleblower claims. During this period, numerous other computer security analysts pointed to flaws in Crowd-Strike's analysis. Among the more interesting were those noting that state security cyber-war typically relies on intercepts, rather than hacks—pointing, as an example, to the famous Russian recording of the Clinton State Department's Victoria Nuland dictating that her "Yats" would replace Yanukovych as Ukraine's leader, in a conversation which included her famous admonition to "fuck the EU." And, it has subsequently been revealed that John Brennan's CIA specialized in false-flag hack operations to hide its own doings.

The biggest and smelliest anomaly in the concocted media narrative however, is the London *Guardian* story of January 7, 2017, and a similar story in the *New York Times*, which noted that British intelligence, specifically GCHQ, "alarmed" about the Trump campaign's "pro-Russian" stance and contacts, tipped off U.S. intelligence that the DNC had been hacked, *back in Autumn of 2015. If that is true, Obama, the DNC, and the FBI knew about the alleged hacks months before revealing them* and, if you believe their own "narrative," did absolutely nothing about them.

10. In October and November, 2016, a new escalation of he Trump/Putin demonization campaign began.

At the same time, FBI Director Comey reopened and then promptly closed the Clinton email investigation based on documents found by the New York Police Department on the personal computer of Anthony Weiner, the sex addict married to Clinton aide Huma Abedin. According to Comey, the FBI miraculously examined over 6,500 emails over the course of a few days and determined that nothing new had been discovered. Again, the FBI Director went completely outside established Justice Department protocols and rules in this election eve process.

With respect to Trump, Christopher Steele's dodgy and salacious dossiers were circulated from the Obama/Clinton opposition research team, including claims that the President-elect engaged in perverse sexual acts while in Russia, and could be blackmailed by Putin as a result. This was accompanied by FBI Director Comey briefing the Group of Eight congressmen (those authorized to hear the nation's deepest secrets), about the FBI counter-intelligence investigation of candidate Trump's campaign. These trusted congressmen, who are regularly blackmailed and neutered as a result of intelligence community surveillance, responded with entirely predictable leaks to the news media. Clinton and official Washington loudly campaigned with the claim that Trump was a "Manchurian candidate," a Putin puppet. By October 29, the untrustworthy Senator Harry Reid had gone before Congress to declare that the FBI was withholding devastating information about the Trump campaign's ties to Russia and that he had received classified briefings about the matter.

11. In an apparent effort to influence the Electoral College vote[5] following the election, the Obama Administration leaked a preliminary intelligence community "assessment" that the Russians had hacked the Democrats' computers and otherwise intervened to swing the election to Donald Trump. At the same time,

---

5. Investigative reporter Robert Parry states that he was contacted by a source in July 2016 who said that Obama and his intelligence chiefs were conspiring to ensure that neither Clinton nor Trump would become President, both being viewed as unacceptable. They hoped that the Clinton email fiasco and Trump Russiagate would result in the emergence of a third choice acceptable to Obama and his spies.

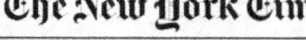

BuzzFeed NEWS

These Reports Allege Trump Has Deep Ties To Russia

...ossier, compiled by a person who has claimed to be a former Bri... ...gence official, alleges Russia has compromising information on ... The allegations are unverified, and the report contains errors.

The New York Tim...

Trump Was Told of Claims Russia Has Damaging Details on Him

LIVE MSNBC

BUZZFEED: DOCUMENTS CLAIM RUSSIA GOVERNMENT AIDED TRUMP FOR YEARS

LIVE MSNBC

the British intelligence dodgy dossiers were widely offered up to the news media, but had so little credibility that most media outlets, who bit on every hysterical morsel fed to them about Trump, refused to publish them.

12. On January 6, 2017, according to James Comey's June 8 congressional testimony, the intelligence chiefs went to Trump Tower to present the Obama Administration's report on Russian hacking, hoping to persuade the skeptical President-elect to abandon his campaign promise for better relations with Putin and Russia. Following that briefing, in a pre-arranged move with the rest of Obama's intelligence directors, Comey cleared the room of everyone but himself and Trump. He presented Trump with the Steele dossier's most salacious allegation, namely that Trump had engaged in sexually perverse acts with Russian prostitutes while visiting Moscow, and that Putin had taped it. This is exactly what the infamous J. Edgar Hoover did—blackmail Washington politicians with FBI dossiers, assuring them that he could protect them so long as they did as Hoover wished. In fact, Comey described this as a " moment" in answers to questions by Senator Susan Collins on June 8.[6]

J. Edgar Hoover

13. Trump appears to have demanded that the entirely fake dossier be investigated, and did not budge about reversing his efforts to achieve better relations with Russia. In fact, Trump denounced the intelligence community publicly as acting like Nazis. He also denounced the McCarthyite hysteria they were generating. While Comey recorded the President-elect's responses on a classified computer moments after leaving him, *Buzzfeed*, which had frequently published raw Clinton/Obama "oppo" stories, published the initial June 2016 British/Clinton dodgy dossier in full. The U.S. intelligence community, particularly Obama's ghoulish grand inquisitor, CIA head John Brennan, proceeded to give it credibility by leaking that both President-elect Trump and President Obama had been briefed on its contents.

14. Publication of the Trump Russian sex allegations were accompanied by the Obama Administration's public presentation of a fact-less "official intelligence community assessment" that the Russians hacked the DNC and Podesta, and that they did so to influence the election in favor of Donald Trump. This "assessment" was put together by analysts hand-picked by Brennan from the NSA, CIA, and FBI, with the NSA voicing only "moderate" confidence that the Russians hacked the election to favor Trump. This

---

6. LaRouche was not the only person to see the parallel to J. Edgar Hoover. See Robert Parry, "'Soft Coup' on Trump Hiding in Plain Sight," *Consortium News*, June 8, 2017.

conclusion was broadcast to the public without any presentation of actual evidence to back it up, and without any obvious reason for the Russians to recklessly provoke Clinton when they and everyone else thought she would be the next President of the United States. Rather than provide facts to back this "assessment" (John Brennan having subsequently explained to Congress and the public that he does not "do evidence"), the appendix to the official report is instead an attack on Russian press outlets, particularly *RT*, for successful "propaganda" efforts in the United States. As we shall see, this targeting, which seemed so McCarthyite and plainly weird at the time, was hardly accidental.

The Democrats, the news media, and their Republican allies, led by John McCain and Lindsey Graham, went berserk with the fact-less Obama Administration "assessment," demanding special prosecutors and congressional investigations, and sneering that "other shoes" were about to drop. Democratic Senator Mark Warner, his voice shaking, and looking in every respect like the overgrown adolescent that he is, solemnly declared that investigating and pimping these fact-less conclusions was the most important moment of his life. Other Democrats and allied media, like the *New York Times'* Thomas Friedman, having clearly lost it, claimed that Russia had committed an "act of war," presumably seeking to invoke Article 5 of the NATO treaty.

15. On March 1, 2017, the *New York Times* revealed that Obama and his national security colleagues had spent the months after the election and prior to President Trump's inauguration dropping a trail of "leads" in official documents and leaking information, in the effort to de-legitimize Trump and to continue their policies against Russia and China.

There were two publicly known and extremely significant Obama Administration actions in this process. On December 24, 2016, Obama signed the National Defense Authorization Act (NDAA), which includes the "Countering Foreign Propaganda and Disinformation Act." It aims to mobilize the entire government, U.S. media, academia, NGOs, and foreign partners and allies to "expose and counter" foreign propaganda and disinformation directed against U.S. national security

C-Span

Former CIA Director John Brennan, testifying on alleged Russian involvement in the 2016 U.S. Presidential election.

interests, and "proactively advance fact-based narratives that support United States allies and interests." The primary target for this black-propaganda, fake-news offensive is the population of the United States. During the Reagan Administration, such activities were called Active Measures and, at least legally, confined to foreign targets.

The NDAA's incredible Orwellian assault on the First Amendment was preceded by a November 25, 2016 *Washington Post* story publishing the names of several media outlets, which it labeled to be Russian propaganda fronts. The list of media outlets smeared as Russian agents was provided by an anonymous group tied to the government and calling itself "Prop or Not." The list included not only *RT* and *Sputnik*, but also *Consortium News*, *Breitbart*, the *Drudge Report*, *Truthout* and other "left" critics of Obama, *AntiWar.com*, and the *Ron Paul Institute*. In short, just about everyone who had criticized the Obama/Clinton war drive against Russia[7] was named, in McCarthyite fashion, as a Russian "propaganda front." Facebook and other social media outlets immediately launched initiatives to censor and curtail "fake news."

Obama complained bitterly throughout the election campaign that Americans had displayed a disturbing

---

7. We have been told by a source that the only reason LaRouche was not on this public list was because entities associated with him had long been subject to active measures under E.O. 12333 by both Bush and Obama.

LIVE
2:55 pm ET

RUSSIA & 2016 ELECTIONS
JAMES CLAPPER
Former Director of National Intelligence
Obama Administration, 2010-17

C-SPAN3
c-span.org
@cspan

C-Span

James Clapper, Obama's Director of National Intelligence, testifying May 8, 2017, on alleged Russian involvement in the 2016 U.S. Presidential election.

propensity to believe the Russians, rather than Obama, on issues of war and peace. This is hardly a shocking development based on *repeated and demonstrable lies* by his and like American administrations concerning the war in Viet Nam, 9/11, the war in Iraq, the war in Syria, the coup in Ukraine, the coup and assassination of Qaddafi in Libya, the terrorist assault on Benghazi, and the mass-surveillance state exposed by Edward Snowden. Based on Obama's bizarre public comments, it appears that he already knew that his administration's active measures program, described by Cass Sunstein as "cognitively infiltrating" the brains of domestic opponents, was simply not working.[8]

Then, on December 15, 2016, DNI James Clapper signed new procedures allowing the NSA to distribute raw intercept data throughout the entire intelligence community. These procedures became official on January 3, 2017, when Attorney General Loretta Lynch signed off on them. The revision had been in the works for over a year. At issue is modification of secret procedures under E.O. 12333, deemed by Edward Snowden and others as the most significant authority for our present, completely unconstitutional surveillance-state. Previously, the NSA was required to filter and redact information regarding U.S. citizens monitored in foreign counterintelligence activities. Thus, officials who have been leaking raw intercept data about Trump to

the national news media could claim some degree of immunity from prosecution under the combined legal impact of the NDAA and the revised E.O. 12333.

All of this dissemination was facilitated by a new cloud intelligence data platform accessible by all intelligence agencies and private contractors, engineered by Clapper and obliterating many paper and digital access trails and safeguards. As a result, searches for leakers became infinitely more difficult.

Most experts on the matter, including former NSA executive William Binney, former Ambassador Jack Matlock, and Colin Powell's former chief of staff, Colonel Lawrence Wilkerson, agree that the most likely source of the avalanche of leaks concerning the Trump campaign transition and initial days in the White House are raw NSA intercepts generated under E.O. 12333 or intercepts by GCHQ, the NSA's British counterpart, which functions under E.O. 12333 without any of the constraints of U.S. law. Britain's GCHQ monitors the entire world's communications channels through the cables on which they pass under the Atlantic. The British press reports that the head of GCHQ appears to have been mysteriously fired right in the midst of the Trump-Russia contretemps.

Congressional investigations have also focused on another source for the leaks: the unmasking by Obama Administration officials of intercepts based on long-standing FISA surveillance targets, such as the Russians. Under FISA procedures, the identities of American citizens caught in otherwise authorized surveillance of foreign targets are to be masked, unless there is a well-articulated reason for unmasking them. It seems clear that Michael Flynn's pre-inauguration conversations with Russian Ambassador Kislyak, which led to Flynn's firing in February, were unmasked in this fashion by Comey's FBI. In April 2017, the FISA Court itself, in a scathing decision, castigated the Obama FBI and other agencies for practices which routinely exposed intercepts of the conversations of American citizens, in direct violation of the Fourth Amendment to the U.S. Constitution.

Various Justice Department and NSA Inspector General reports, and reports of DNI Clapper, state that Obama Administration officials unmasked Americans'

8. See T. Papert, "Obama Aide Sunstein Outlines Plan to Suppress Opposition," *EIR*, May 11, 2012.

United States Army Lieutenant General Michael Flynn (ret.), at a campaign rally in Arizona.

conversations with foreign targets at an alarming and unparalleled rate.

16. Following General Flynn's firing in February and a deluge of leaks of classified surveillance disclosing every interaction with the Russians and other transition team and national defense matters, on March 4, 2017, President Trump interrupted the entire fake media narrative by tweeting what had become obvious: that Obama had him "wiretapped" in Trump Tower prior to the election, and that what was happening to him reeked of McCarthyism. The media, which had been publishing allegations about FISA warrants and intercepts of Trump or his associates for months, erupted in what has to be one the largest and most shameless demonstrations of the Big Lie ever known. They declared that Trump was offering wild claims with no evidence, essentially circling back on their very own reporting and labeling it, "fake news."

As has been the case throughout the media's war on Trump, the Tweet was deconstructed to its most literal and bizarre potential meaning. The media focused on the literal term "wiretapped," declaring that the President was off his rocker and making unsubstantiated claims to the American public. By the media's bizarre rendition, the President meant that Barack Obama himself surreptitiously entered Trump Tower and placed a physical tap on Trump's personal phones. In the resulting propaganda torrent, Trump's reasonable and truthful conclusion, that his presidential campaign and its associates were unlawfully surveilled by the Obama Administration and that he was a victim of McCarthyism, was deliberately obscured by a new daily fake news cycle. Presumably, the media hoped that the public had the attention span of a gnat and would simply forget the media's own claims which they, themselves, had relentlessly reported.

17. On March 20, 2017, former FBI Director Comey breathed new life into what was, by then, an operation against Trump that had begun to flag. People were simply tired of Democrats, like Adam Schiff,[9] trying on McCarthyite tin-foil hats before TV cameras and pontificating about the outrage *du jour.* Comey, in testimony before the House Select Committee on Intelligence, made it officially public, for the first time, that the FBI had been investigating collusion between the Trump campaign and Russian interference in the election since July 2016. He opined that the FBI counterintelligence investigation (which had been leaking like a sieve since its instigation in July, without producing any verifiable facts about either Russian interference or Trump campaign collusion in the same) could continue for many more months, if not years. He refused to say whether the President himself was under investigation, despite the fact that he had told the President this and had told Congress the same thing behind closed doors.

18. Despite the daily press instructions about events which the public must view as "scandalous," and highly publicized congressional hearings—concerning Russia! Russia! Russia!—all of President Obama's men, at this late date, had only managed to arrange the human sacrifice of Michael Flynn for lying to the Vice President about his conversations with the Russian am-

---

9. Schiff looks every bit like a mixture between Charlie Brown and a Conehead, with the grasping and crazy personality of Lucy Van Pelt. As a prosecutor it took him three tries to convict the hapless former FBI agent Richard Miller of espionage, despite overwhelming and salacious evidence.

bassador in December.[10] They had also generated ethics, foreign intelligence registration, and tax questions about their other Trump campaign targets, typical of what happens when an entire life is put under a microscope in a dedicated search for something, anything, that could be construed feasibly as wrongdoing. Ask yourself, what have any of these people allegedly done? Spoken with the Russians? Talked about lifting sanctions imposed because Putin reacted to a coup Obama ran against the duly elected government of Ukraine? Lobbied on behalf of foreign governments? Really?

19. Up to this point, the congressional inquiries were also a national embarrassment, as British-controlled operatives droned on and on to straight-faced U.S. senators about how "thousands" of pesky Russian computer nerds had engineered Hillary Clinton's defeat by using bots to post negative but truthful news about Clinton on Americans' social media accounts. They claimed that this practice "weaponized" information: To wit, tiny bullets composed solely of facts had been aimed at the American collective mind, creating an alien result.[11]

The actual testimony of Obama's intelligence officials was buried amidst these bizarre claims and other media hype. Each of them testified that there was absolutely no evidence of any Trump campaign collusion with Russian efforts to interfere in the U.S. elections. In fact, on March 15, 2017, Comey himself had told Senators Chuck Grassley and Diane Feinstein behind closed doors, that the President was not a target of his investigations, despite planted press stories to the contrary. Comey had otherwise continually stone-walled Grassley concerning the senator's persistent questions about the FBI's relationship to British operative Christopher Steele.

---

10. Flynn's scalping itself was the result of the unmasking of Flynn's name and illegal leaks of the same to the press as a result of classified surveillance. This fact was obliterated by sensational press coverage of the hyperventilated visit of Obama Assistant Attorney General Sally Yates to the White House to warn, nonsensically, that Flynn had been "compromised" by the Russians because he lied to the Vice-President. Exactly how this makes any sense at all we have not been told. As King Lear remarked, "it is a tale, told by an idiot, full of sound and fury, signifying nothing."

11. Hillary Clinton recently rounded this out by claiming that voters had been bombed with "cognitive dissonance." The world awaits her details, which surely involve Putin renting a crop-duster plane, loading it with this dissonance, and dusting the entire former industrial heartland.

The headlines and conversation in the nation's heartland have increasingly mocked official Washington, popularly labeling Russiagate so much "bullshit," and more eloquently claiming it is an overheated and paranoid journey in search of a completely unarticulated and missing crime—sort of a repeat of Colonel Jack D. Ripper in the *Dr. Strangelove* movie obsessed with the idea that the Russians have somehow stolen "our precious bodily fluids." The rest of the world, aside from the Madhatter British, Germans, and French, and their controlled satraps, think this country has flipped its collective lid, finding the President, based on conversations with him, to be a very serious and concerned human being, someone they can finally talk to.

While unable to produce any saleable legal goods, the illicit investigations have significantly bogged down the President's political agenda, while fostering an increasingly toxic and divisive national political environment. The strategy of Obama and his British friends is clear: split cowardly Republicans away from Trump, whom they didn't really support in the first place. Hope that the President's silent majority remains exactly that—silent. Hope that some of the smelly stuff they are throwing up against the wall actually sticks. Distract, distract, distract the President and prevent him from working with Russia and China to develop the world, end wars, and implement the massive infrastructure and space exploration projects that will actually save our economy.

20. On May 3, 2017, Comey followed his March drama-queen performance before the House with even more theatrical speechifying before the Senate Judiciary Committee. He bloviated that despite the fact that his unprecedented disclosures and handling of the Clinton email investigation may have impacted the election, and made him nauseous, he, Mr. Eagle Scout and True Crime Detective rolled into one, would do the same thing all over again. He exaggerated the significance of the Anthony Weiner computer discovery by stating that it contained thousands of new Clinton emails, not previously produced, some of which were classified—a statement the FBI had to subsequently correct. He refused to state publicly that President Trump was not under investigation, despite repeatedly assuring the President of that, allowing the media and Democratic party color revolution to continue. He refused to confirm that there was any investigation into the torrent of illegal classified leaks at the center of the media campaign.

21. On May 9, President Trump fired Comey. The insurrection against the President now is supposed to enter a new phase, following a familiar Washington legal playbook. Absent any crime, an alleged coverup now is supposed to become the legal and media focus.

II. Who is James Comey?

From here, the story will only get stranger than it already has. Make no mistake about it, both Comey and newly appointed Special Prosecutor, Robert Mueller, viewed as "serious people" by official Washington and the treasonous media, are nothing but longstanding legal thugs now out to do the President in.

Comey's "straight arrow" reputation fantasy, puffed endlessly by the press, involves Mueller and him facing down the Bush Administration in 2004 at the bedside of the gravely ill Attorney General John Ashcroft. The Bushies wanted reauthorization of the illegal NSA Steller Wind surveillance program. Then Bush Deputy Attorney General Comey and FBI Director Mueller prevented Bush's White House from getting Ashcroft's okay from his hospital bed.

To make sure everyone "got" just how incredibly courageous he had been, Comey arranged to retell the story at a Senate Judiciary hearing in May 2007, choreographing the entire episode with Democratic Senator Chuck Schumer and Schumer's then aide and Comey bro, Preet Bharara. Comey's dramatic rendition of events left out the fact that Stellar Wind was reauthorized, with some cosmetic legal changes, a few weeks after his visit to Ashcroft's hospital bed. Comey otherwise legally signed off on waterboarding, rendition, and other Bush war crimes, but now claims to have secretly opposed "torture" in internal Bush Administration deliberations.

After his stint at Main Justice, Comey spent five years as General Counsel for Lockheed Martin, the Pentagon's largest contractor. Many name Lockheed as a key Deep State player in Washington's military-cen-

fbi.gov

Former Director of the Federal Bureau of Investigation, James Comey.

tered scheme for national economic production.[12] After five years at Lockheed, Comey spent three years at Bridgewater Associates, the largest hedge-fund in the world. Featuring a culture of New Age "complete transparency" between all of its managers and employees, coupled with Wall Street's brand of satanic social Darwinism, Bridgewater has been described as a cult by former employees. It recruits heavily from Ivy League colleges, with the addition of former spooks from the CIA and NSA.

After Bridgewater, and shortly before his appointment by Obama to be Director of the FBI, Comey joined the board of the notorious Hong Kong and Shanghai Banking Corporation (HSBC), the historic British Crown bank for drug-money laundering and intelligence operations. HSBC was created to finance Britain's opium war against China, and has functioned as a laundromat for British drug and other dirty money operations for more than a century.[13] He joined HSBC after the Obama Justice Department signed a highly controversial and disgusting Deferred Prosecution Agreement (DPA) with the bank in December 2012

---

12. See Mike Lofgren, *The Deep State*, Penguin, New York, 2016.
13. See *Dope, Inc., The Book that Drove Kissinger Crazy*, EIR, Washington, D.C., 1992.

for multiple criminal acts involving drug and other illicit funds which critics rightly called a corrupt "slap on the wrist." Investigators rightly believed that HSBC officials should have been criminally prosecuted and the Bank should have been shut down. Comey was hired to help HSBC, involved in criminal activities for decades, appear to comply with the DPA and fend off the independent outside monitor policing compliance. Predictably the outside monitor reported to the Court in January 2015, that "historical cultural deficiencies continued to pervade HSBC's operations."

Following his firing, Comey and friends leaked to the press notes which he had allegedly taken following most of his encounters with the President. With each encounter, Comey's leaked account says, he returned to discuss what was said and its implications with a close circle of his FBI comrades. He prepared for each encounter with the President based on "murder boards" conducted by his FBI colleagues. In the course of their meetings, Comey says, the President asked for his loyalty, portraying this like the request of some mafia don in a bad Hollywood movie. If it happened, such a request, in the context of what appeared to be an open insurrection against the President by the intelligence community, is hardly surprising. The President denies that it happened.

On the day after the President fired Flynn, according to Comey, the President cleared the room and went one-on-one with him, expressing the "hope" that Comey could let the matter of Michael Flynn go. Comey whines that he took the President's "hope" as an "order" giving rise to concerns about possible obstruction of justice. This line of reasoning was thoroughly eviscerated by Senator James Risch on June 8, getting Comey to admit that Trump never ordered him, only expressed "hope," and that no prosecution that Comey knew of ever went forward based on someone expressing "hope" for something. While the President denies this ever happened, Harvard Law Professor Emeritus and famed trial lawyer Alan Dershowitz writes that the President would be fully within his legal and constitutional prerogatives to order Comey to back off from Flynn. He could have simply told Comey, legally, "I am going to pardon Flynn."

It should be clear that Comey was trying to set the President up, to entrap him, an escapade which was "crudely" interrupted when the President fired him.

Comey confirmed as much in his Congressional testimony, telling Senator Susan Collins that the reason why he did not stop the President from improper interactions if he thought they were such, the reason he concealed the alleged improper and possibly illegal conduct from his superiors at the Justice Department, the reason he did not resign, was because his encounters with the President were of "investigative interest" to the FBI. Otherwise, Comey's leaks reveal a man so leery of even shaking the President's hand (or being photographed doing so) that once in January he tried to hide himself in the White House drapes in the hope that Trump would not see him.

The problem with this new soap opera, is that both Comey and his Assistant Andrew McCabe have previously testified, under oath, to Congress, that there was no pressure to end the FBI's investigations from anyone in the Trump Administration. And, Comey confirmed in his testimony that prior to his firing, Trump was not under investigation for collusion with Russia, obstruction, or any other offense. Further, Comey has proved that he is willing to violate professional norms and Justice Department regulations, if not laws, by leaking government documents. The question is, what else was leaked by Comey and his FBI circle?[14]

Perhaps the capper in the media leaks about Comey, however, is a *Washington Post* story claiming that Comey received a report from an FBI source in March 2016, stating that the Russians had email correspondence between Attorney General Loretta Lynch, Debra Wasserman Schultz, and another prominent Democratic fundraiser. In the alleged and probably non-existent email, Lynch provided assurances that the Clinton email investigation would not get far.

Despite the fact that Comey's own FBI concluded that the alleged email was fake and the FBI never got its hands on it, Comey insisted that the fake and probably non-existent Russian email was a major factor in his decision to hold his own extraordinary and illicit public press conference closing the Clinton email investigation and discussing raw evidence.

Okay. So, rather than listening to his guy, shouldn't Congress be questioning his mental state? Did FBI Director Comey, rather than Russia, actually meddle in our elections because the FBI director indulged himself

---

14. See Jonathan Turley, "The Case Against James Comey," *The Hill*, June 9, 2017.

in a paranoid anti-Putin, frenzied fantasy? Why is the media jumping all over the President for calling this guy "nuts?"

III. Who is Robert Mueller?

Those familiar with the relationship between Comey and Robert Mueller describe them as "joined at the hip," "cut from the same cloth" (can't help thinking of the Union Jack), close personal friends, and mentor (Mueller) and mentee (Comey). The problem with this relationship is that Department of Justice conflict guidelines specifically bar prosecutors (Mueller) from investigating issues where close friends (Comey) have a significant role, such as material witnesses. Official Washington knows all of this and yet touts this investigation as somehow "independent" and "apolitical."

Robert Mueller's claims to fame involve various outrageous services conducted on behalf of the Bush family and the British. He was the "legal brain" in the Boston prosecution of Lyndon LaRouche, employing a former avowed satanist, John Markham, as the lead attorney on that case.[15] (I kid you not.) Mueller's prosecution featured an investigation initiated under the auspices of E.O. 12333 and involving many still-classified operations, together with a national media defamation onslaught engineered by CIA and Bush operative John Train, followed by a military occupation of the town of Leesburg, Virginia, an attempt to provoke a shootout assassination under the auspices of a search warrant, and numerous black bag jobs, infiltrations, and planted and false trial evidence. Mueller's Boston prosecution collapsed when trial judge Robert Keeton ruled that the government had engaged in "institutional and systemic misconduct."[16]

Former Director of the Federal Bureau of Investigation, Robert Mueller III.

Public Domain

Former U.S. Attorney General Ramsey Clark, who represented LaRouche on appeal, said the LaRouche case "represented a broader range of deliberate cunning and systematic misconduct over a longer period of time utilizing the power of the Federal government than any other prosecution by the U.S. government in my time and to my knowledge."

Needless to say, Mueller does not reference the LaRouche prosecution as a career highlight. Instead he cites the prosecution of Manuel Noriega and the Lockerbie bombing case, both of which involved covering up for George H.W. Bush. In the Noriega case, it was covering up the cocaine financing connected to Bush's Contra operations that was at issue. Manuel Noriega refused to cooperate in that Bush drug-running scheme but knew so much about it that he became a liability. A U.S. invasion was arranged, lots of people were killed, and a highly corrupt prosecution took place.[17] In Lockerbie, an arrangement between Bush and Margaret Thatcher to blame the bombing on Libya and cover for U.S. intelligence activities was at stake.

As Director of the FBI, Mueller was a key architect of the surveillance and propaganda state now dominant in the United States following 9/11. It was in that context that he provided perhaps his most deeply appreciated personal service for the Bush family, covering up for Saudi involvement in the 9/11 murders of 3,000 Americans. The 9/11 families and former U.S. Senator Bob Graham cite Mueller as the key figure in this coverup.

EIR, March 10, 2000. After Boston, the prosecution was shipped off to Alexandria, Virginia, where long-time deep-state operative Judge Albert J. Bryan, Jr., waited to do the government's bidding. To manufacture the loan "fraud" case against LaRouche, the government instigated what was later ruled an illegal and bad-faith bankruptcy, preventing LaRouche entities from servicing or paying political loans. Judge Bryan barred any reference to the government-instigated bankruptcy during LaRouche's Alexandria trial.

17. See, e.g., Jonathan Marshall, "Missing the Real Noriega Story," *Consortium News*, June 1, 2017.

---

15. Markham's early legal career involved services for, and membership in the satanic Process Church of the Final Judgement cult.
16. See 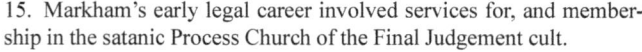 "USA v. LaRouche, 'He's a Bad Guy But We Can't Say Why.'"

IV. So, Now You Know

Since the election and before, we have been stuck in a very elaborate and dangerous British hoax, gambling the future of our nation. If you look at it closely, you see how absurd it really is. Already, across the world, a new reality has emerged. Russia, China, now Japan, and sixty-eight other nations are engaged in China's One Belt, One Road Great Project, the largest infrastructure project in human history. Over the last forty years, Lyndon LaRouche, with his wife, Helga Zepp-La-Rouche, have worked tirelessly to provide the world with the type of bold economic development initiatives and great projects capable of lifting the human race from infancy to adulthood, from backwardness and poverty to the riches of creative discovery and productivity, shared across all cultures.

Against the screams daily emanating from the controlled media and the men and women of Davos, an actual engine for economic growth has been unleashed on the world. This engine is moving inexorably forward, governed by a new paradigm for mankind. In light of this development, the fate of the Anglo-American coup plotters is like that of so many smelly dinosaurs. They have doomed themselves because they cannot escape the failed and evil paradigm in which they have encased themselves. They fight desperate battles in a war where victory has already been won, in reality, by the other side. Unleashing a wave of hope throughout the developing world, China's Great Project could, if joined by the United States, usher in a new, boundless, human renaissance and make Donald Trump the greatest President in U.S. history.

Since September 2013, China has undertaken a huge infrastructure building project ripe with the potential to transform entire underdeveloped, forsaken, or war ravaged areas of the Earth into modern, beautiful cities and productive economies. It is now being built. Russia, China, and also India, have turned their imaginations, at the same time, to near space exploration, intent on exploring and developing the Moon where, among other wonders, the possibility for rapid development of fusion energy to power the Earth and future space travel beckons.

China's President Xi Jinping asked the United States to join this effort; Barack Obama adamantly refused, continuing a series of hostile actions which can only be described as a New Cold War. As opposed to Obama and his brutish Atlanticist buddies, Donald Trump has formed a personal bond with President Xi and sent a U.S. delegation to China's historic May 14-15, 2017 Belt and Road Summit. That summit also featured a major address by Helga Zepp-LaRouche, who was welcomed with great respect and recognition of the ideas and campaigns she has waged, with her husband, for the common good of mankind.

The Democrats who are leading the insurrection against Trump are very, very weak. An amalgam of parochial and identity-politics special interests—gays, suburban professional women, Hollywood entertainment figures, upwardly-mobile minorities, environmentalists, students, and the professional class of lawyers, accountants, journalists, and techies—now constitute the Democratic Party's base.[18] The working class, other producers, and farmers have been dumped entirely. The country's producers yearn to participate in the new paradigm of human productivity. The amalgam of forces arrayed against the President only can manage the feeble color revolution slogan, "resist"—they have no program. They have no vision for the future. Similarly, many of the Republicans who now constrain and undermine the President, are stuck squarely in the old paradigm, insisting on austerity and "small government" to reward Wall Street and continue the casino economy.

Since Obama's election in 2008, a parallel structure built from that election has dominated Democratic politics. State chairs and traditional Democratic Party constituency leaders were largely ignored. The "working class" was abandoned in favor of an army of professionals and the entitled, all wrapped in the Hollywood glitz and glamor essential to Barack Obama's endless preening and self-love. Significant funding was put into training professional organizers for Organizing for Action, Move On, the Working Families Party, and other entities, by the billionaires of the Democracy Alliance, which includes George Soros as only one of its billionaire donors.

This Obama/Democratic Leadership Council formation has left the Democratic Party in the worst shape of its entire historical existence. It has lost the Presidency, both houses of Congress, and almost every gov-

---

18. Both Thomas Frank, in his book, *Listen Liberal* (Picador, New York, 2016), and Christopher Lasch in his last book, *Revolt of the Elites* (W.W. Norton, New York, 1995) describe this mix of the elite and the entitled as the fatal, final blow to the party of Franklin Roosevelt. Trump advisor Steve Bannon has described Lasch's work as one of his favorite books.

White House

President Trump speaking about his Infrastructure Initiative on June 7, 2017 near Cincinnati, Ohio.

cago exploded in drug and gang related murders.[19] There is a limit to how long you can spit in peoples' faces and call it rain.

The way is clear for the President to win. The population must mobilize, as La-Rouche said, and tell their senators and congressmen to cut it out, stop the coup, and jail its perpetrators before this great country is destroyed. Under our Constitution, the people have the unique capability to stop a coup, by kicking their senators and representatives in the ass, and not accepting "no" for an answer. Tell your congressman and the President to join the One Belt, One Road project and implement LaRouche's Four Laws for recovery of the United States. Show the population this great vision for the future as Franklin Roosevelt once did; mobilize the population directly for this program and tell Republican and Democratic Wall Street pawns, whether they are spouting Von Hayek and Milton Friedman or John Maynard Keynes, to get out of the way. The Gods of Olympus may scream and yell and attempt to hurl lightning bolts, but, as a result of the economic revival now underway in the Pacific and Eurasia, the ground under Mount Olympus is rapidly giving way. The would-be emperors have shown us that they have no clothes, and that they are really quite insane. They now can be ridiculed, mocked, and laughed at, something everyone should do daily. As Martin Luther King so eloquently noted, economic and social progress are the true measures of any society—the true mandate of Heaven. That reality is on our side.

ernorship in the United States. At the donors' meetings which led to the present "resist" mobilization, it is reliably reported that the donors, fearing a complete split by Sanders supporters, who wanted real change and had been repeatedly kicked in the face by the Democrats-In-Name-Only Obama apparatus, settled on the "resist" color revolution strategy as a matter of pure survival.

As Trump rightly insists, all of the theater we are witnessing has nothing to do with why Hillary Clinton lost the election. Hillary Clinton sealed her fate by calling Trump voters a racist, misogynist "basket of deplorables." She adamantly refused to address the economic depression prevalent everywhere except the enclaves of the professional and elite classes on the nation's coasts, sticking to the demographic data computer scenarios utilized by Obama. She campaigned against Glass-Steagall and tied herself completely to Barack Obama's failed legacy. Clinton's criminal idiocy was echoed by Barack Obama himself, who speechified about how he created an economic recovery—a declaration made as the U.S. death rate soared among boomers and gen-Xers, as most former industrial states battled a drug and suicide epidemic and whole sections of his former organizing turf in Chi-

---

19. *EIR* detailed the dismal results of "community control" and similar Alinskyite organizing in 1979, citing a series by reporter Roy Harvey that showed how a Field Foundation operation in Chicago exploded into violence by the gangs being manipulated in a human social experiment. "The Gangs—Who Benefits," *EIR*, four-part series, Aug. 7, 14, and 28, and Sept. 11, 1979. The same gang/drug gang violence is responsible for Chicago's horrendous murder rate today.

IV. What Do We Actually Mean by `Infrastructure'

APRIL 17, 2010

WHAT YOUR ACCOUNTANT NEVER UNDERSTOOD

The Secret Economy

by Lyndon H. LaRouche, Jr.

A prefatory comment on the implications of the subject of the following report:

Fortunately, at least a relatively few leading talents among U.S. economists have understood certain essentials of "the how and why" of my uniquely successful record in economic forecasting, that since 1956-57, to the present date. Unfortunately, many other economists have not yet understood this. The root of the failures by the relatively larger number of economists, as shown by virtually all accountants, and all but a few leading economists, is that they are, essentially, worshipful victims of a widely taught delusion, known as **monetarism***: the worship of an imagined monetary "magic of the marketplace," their foolish belief in money as such.*

Therefore, the relevant questions include: "What is the secret? Why have most among the world's presently leading economists, been so stubbornly incompetent, for so long, in matters pertaining to forecasting of the medium- to long-term patterns of net, **physical-economic** *development, in both the relevant nation, and in the world at large? Why has the U.S. economy been in a trend of an actually measurable,* **physical-economic** *decline, actually, since the day after the death of President Franklin D. Roosevelt?"*

The related problem of the present U.S. Federal Government, is, essentially, the same presented by the case of the crazed Roman Emperor Nero: like Nero, our current President, Obama, is feared for the power he wields (however temporarily), although the policies of that British puppet and would-be quasi-emperor, Obama, would, if continued, doom the world as a whole, economically and otherwise. Thus, today, as

The U.S. Congress leaps in the footsteps of the sheep of François Rabelais's Panurge. Said the merchant Dindenault: "Suddenly . . . Panurge threw his sheep, crying and bleating, into the sea. All the other sheep, crying and bleating in the same intonation, started to throw themselves in the sea after it, all in a line. The herd was such that once one jumped, so jumped its companions. It was not possible to stop them; as you know, with sheep, it's natural to always follow the first one, wherever it may go." Drawing by Gustave Doré.

long as Obama's ideology remains in office, the delusion called "monetarism" will have driven nations, even continents of the world, into the verge of a "lemming-like" self-destruction, as by, most notably the Democratic Party's sheepish majority in the U.S. Congress.

Baaa!

The consequent results experienced in today's trans-Atlantic economy, should suffice to convince those who are still sane, to reconsider those presumptions of British Liberalism which have sent the U.S.A. and the European economies plunging, since mid-2007, into their presently accelerating state of physical collapse.

The U.S. economy could be saved, even at this late stage of its perilous decline, that through the application of the combination of a "Glass-Steagall" reform of the U.S.A., especially if combined with the same cleansing of other leading nations, by the Glass-Steagall method, when it is applied to create a return of leading other nations to a Franklin-Roosevelt form of fixed-exchange-rate system.

Thus, as the result of a decades-long process of virtual ridding of sane U. S. traditions from the practice of our U.S. government, the key to the possibility for saving the United States from total ruin now, is the fact that I have a decades-long record of being a remarkably successful physical economist, an economist for whom the subject of economics is a branch of physical science, rather than what is presented as the popular, monetarist delusions taught and practiced as a failed system of financial accounting masquerading as economics. I know what I am doing; therefore, I must warn, that your nation's survival depends on your understanding these differences now.

Introduction: 'On Mere Money'

The remedy for the world's presently onrushing economic collapse, lies, uniquely, in the replacement of the currently prevalent world monetary systems, by *a Franklin Roosevelt type of combination of Glass-Steagall standards for nations' credit systems within a global, fixed-exchange-rate system.* This can succeed, if the implementation of the reform is crafted from the standpoint of an actual, but still rarely-taught, and little known subject: *the physical science of political economy.*

That subject represents a body of actually scientific knowledge which presents, in a unique way, the systemic distinction of the human being from all the lower forms of life. The power of that knowledge, is the source of the effect of the distinction between what V.I. Vernadsky named "the Biosphere," and what he named "the Noösphere."

So, on the same subject of scientific method, as Albert Einstein had shown for the case of Johannes Kepler's uniquely original discovery of the principle of universal gravitation, as in Kepler's **The Harmonies of the Worlds**, all nature is "creative," in what Einstein identified as Kepler's *finite but unbounded universe,* (in other words, inherently an *anti-entropic, universal* process). This means that the individual human being is set apart from, and above all other forms of life, that by the human individual's potential for the role of willful human creativity in producing that special quality of anti-entropic effect which is to be recognized as mankind's willful quality of superiority over all other known living species.

In the real universe, money as such has no intrinsic value. Money is properly used, not as a standard of real economic value, but, as under our U.S. Federal Constitution, as a convenient medium of, not value, but, the conveying of a form of credit uttered by a sovereign republic, credit which is to be deployed to promote an effect which is intended to be identified as *increased net physical value per capita and per square kilometer of territory for the economy as a whole.* Money, when so defined, performs its proper function only through promoting increasingly productive, capital-intensive investment, per capita and per square kilometer, in both basic economic infrastructure, and in methods of production for the long-term development of the more highly productive, more advanced technologies, as since the mid-Seventeenth-century Commonwealth of Massachusetts operating under its Charter. This means developments which both (1.) *must offset the effects of attrition*, and (2.) *which represent, in effect, a method of discovery expressed as a physical net increase in the human species' expanded power to continue to exist into an unbounded future, as per capita and per square kilometer of relevant territory.*

In other words, the survival of humanity always demands an increase in the level of *energy-flux-density* deployed to the effect of accelerating the increase of the productive powers of labor, and, as the role of chlorophyll illustrates that point in the *upward development of the increased role of the relevant carbon* in the consumption by society. So, today so far, an increasingly silly trans-Atlantic society is disintegrating, that through a virtually mass-suicidal reliance on modes of power confined to low levels of energy-flux density, whereas, despite the follies of those British-controlled Russian influentials whose special interests are rooted, personally, among the contemporary financial pirates of the Caribbean, Russia (otherwise), China, and India, are exemplary of the relatively saner nations, as nations relying, more and more, upon nuclear and thermonuclear power, and vast complexes of modernized infrastructure, and comparable types of very high energy-flux-density sources of power.

That power of creativity on which a society's progress, and even survival, depends, is expressed most clearly in what can be identified as Classical forms of artistic composition, as this point is illustrated by the role of Albert Einstein's violin in the function of his often astonishingly great, creative-scientific powers, the same creative powers to be witnessed in the case of the adversaries of Einstein, as Einstein's work is to be contrasted there with that depravity known as modern *mathematical positivism*, a positivism typified at its worst by the followers of Bertrand Russell's operations based in the Cambridge school of "systems analysis."

Typical of the anti-scientific depravity of Russell's dupes, is the case of the Laxenberg, Austria-based International Institute for Applied Systems Analysis (IIASA). IIASA is typified by those notable adversaries of a competent modern science: the adversaries of the competent science which, is, itself, typified by the work of exemplary physical chemists such as the U.S.A.'s William Draper Harkins, Russia's and the Ukraine's Academician V.I. Vernadsky, and their like.

Against that background in the matter of "energy policies," my heretofore unique, decades-spanning successes as a forecaster in the field of the branch of physical science known as "physical economy," have depended, essentially, on the impact, upon me, of the revolution effected by a great successor of both Johannes Kepler and Gottfried Leibniz, and also Carl F. Gauss, that Bernhard Riemann who has been the chief instigator of all of the most crucial of those qualitative improvements in scientific method which are notable historically since Riemann's famous, pace-setting, 1854 habilitation dissertation delivered at Germany's Göttingen University.

So, my exceptional success as an economist has depended greatly on the contributions such as those which are to be found in the work of some among the greatest scientific geniuses of the Twentieth Century, who are typified by such as Max Planck, William Draper Harkins, V.I. Vernadsky, and Albert Einstein, all of whom have depended upon those benefits of Riemann's revolution which are rooted in the conceptions of a modern physical science of not "mathematical physics," nor merely chemistry, but a physical chemistry. The work of these figures of science, is based upon that Riemannian revolution's relationship not only to the preceding work which had been accomplished by Carl Gauss, but is to be credited to the emphasis on the role of Classical artistic creativity by Riemann's teacher and immediate predecessor at Göttingen, who had also been Riemann's professor at Berlin, Alexander von Humboldt's special protégé, Lejeune Dirichlet.[1]

At the beginning, all of what have become my own, relatively unmatched successes in economic forecasting, were rooted in my early adolescent recognition of the intrinsic absurdity of what is known as Euclidean geometry. The need to supersede that reductionist system of ancient Euclid and comparable cases, by *a principle of physical geometry*, was, fortunately, first demonstrated for me, during my adolescence, in repeated weekend visits to the Boston, Massachusetts area's Charlestown U.S. Navy Yard. In these visits, my attention was caught, repeatedly, by the way in which the optimal geometry of physical mass, defined a ratio of supporting structure to total mass, for ongoing cases of high-rise construction based on modern steel. The Eiffel Tower in Paris illustrates the same point, by posing the issue of such optimization in construction in a physical space-time defined in terms of the chronol-

---

1. Since scientific creativity respecting matters of scientific as well as Classical artistic essentials, is rooted in the faculties of Classical artistic composition of architecture, Classical painting, and Classical modes of poetry and music (as distinct from the worse than useless "popular" varieties of today) one must come to an understanding of the relationship of scientific creativity to the fundamental principles underlying Classical artistic composition, such as those of exemplars such as Abraham Kästner, Gotthold Lessing, Moses Mendelssohn, Johann Sebastian Bach, Wolfgang Mozart, Friedrich Schiller, Ludwig van Beethoven, and the circles of Moses Mendelssohn's grandchildren, which included Dirichlet's wife, Rebecca, and her brother Felix. Classical music and poetry are among the most critical sources of inspiration to creative scientific minds, such as that of Albert Einstein, out of the culture marked by the influence of Friedrich Schiller, in Nineteenth-century Germany. This is contrasted to the methods of positivists, such as David Hilbert, and the sterility which is associated with positivist influences on science generally.

Riemann's Crucial Insight

From Bernhard Riemann's habilitation dissertation, On the Hypotheses Which Lie at the Foundations of Geometry, *translated by Henry S. White, in David Eugene Smith, ed.,* **A Source Book in Mathematics** (New York: Dover Publications, 1959):

It is well known that geometry presupposes not only the concept of space but also the first fundamental notions for constructions in space as given in advance. It gives only nominal definitions for them, while the essential means of determining them appear in the form of axioms. The relation of these presuppositions is left in the dark; one sees neither whether and in how far their connection is necessary, nor a priority whether it is possible.

From Euclid to Legendre, to name the most renowned of modern writers on geometry, this darkness has been lifted neither by the mathematicians nor by the philosophers who have labored upon it. The reason of this lay perhaps in the fact that the general concept of multiply extended magnitudes, in which spatial magnitudes are comprehended, has not been elaborated at all. Accordingly I have proposed to myself at first the problem of constructing the concept of a multiply extended magnitude out of general notions of quantity....

[In conclusion:] This path leads out into the domain of another science, into the realm of physics, into which the nature of this present occasion forbids us to penetrate.

ogy of physical chemistry.[2]

The methods of long-range economic forecasting which have provided me the distinguishing, later successes of my work as an economist, were based on a perspective rooted, since early 1953, in my joyous adoption of the method represented by Bernhard Riemann's 1854 habilitation dissertation, a dissertation which is to be read as being the relevant consequence of the leading discoveries by Gottfried Leibniz. On this account, the opening two paragraphs, and concluding single sentence of that habilitation dissertation, are the most notable points of reference for summation of the essential approach to understanding his dissertation's revolution in modern physical science. Those three, selected paragraphs of the habilitation dissertation,[3] summarize the clearing away of the rubbish from the field on which the edifice of his profound contributions, based upon the remaining portions of that dissertation, onward, is erected.

As a Matter of Economy

Notably, my first formal forecast for the U.S. economy, was made, in the Summer of 1956, in the setting of my role as an executive of a consulting firm, during a time when I had forecast the near certainty of the outbreak of the most severe recession of the post-war period thus far, as to occur during the February-March 1957 interval, exactly as it did, in fact;[4] that deepest, prolonged recession of the post-war period up to that time, erupted at exactly that forecast point. Virtually all of my forecasts uttered later, have been of a medium- to long-term character, such as my 1966-1968 forecast of a highly probable breakdown in the existing fixed-exchange-rate system, by "about the end of the 1960s or the beginning of the 1970s."

The success of that latter method for forecasting, led to the crucial and celebrated Queens College debate between me and the noted Liberal economist Abba Lerner, on December 2, 1971, a debate whose essential features have marked the main lines of the course of the economic history of our United States, from that moment to the present day.

---

2. Filippo Brunelleschi's employment of the catenary as a principle of construction of the cupola of *Santa Maria del Fiore*, is an example of this from the roots of modern physical science.

3. "On the Subject of the Hypotheses Which Underlie the Foundations of Geometry."

4. None of my forecasts were ever premised on what is termed "statistical probability," but on specific elements of trends in adopted policies of practice. The relevant type of argument is: "this will probably happen, if a currently likely policy remains operative." Those who rely on such foolishness as, "On a scale of ten, ..." disgust me.

The failures which may be fairly identified as those of my notable rivals in medium- to long-term economic forecasting, have been failures which usually occurred as a consequence of the typical monetarist's reliance on what continue to be inherently incompetent, "statistical" ("show me the money!") modes of so-called "market forecasting."

In seeking the blame for the failures of "market economics," put special emphasis on the disastrous performance of forecasts designed to conform to the ideologies of such followers of the notorious Bertrand Russell as the Professor Norbert Wiener and John v. Neumann, both of whom the famous mathematical positivist David Hilbert quite rightly threw out of Göttingen University's program for reason of their manifestly insufferable incompetence. The scientifically farcical work of John v. Neumann and Oskar Morgenstern on economy, is typical of the rubbish which was attacked on this account, during the late 1950s, as by me, and by such among my contemporaries of that time as Wassily Leontief. Such follies of those and other positivists drawn from the ranks of Bertrand Russell's radically positivist dupes, such as the dupes of the pseudo-scientific cult known as IIASA,[5] are typical of the lunacy respecting economic doctrines of practice, from the time of the death of President Franklin Roosevelt, to the present date.

What Must Be Said, Repeatedly

The typical failures of my contemporary, putative professional rivals' forecasting, reveal their blunders, as blunders which find their root in that empiricist presumption by the followers of Paolo Sarpi which permeates modern monetarist and social dogma. That is the dogma which is most frequently associated with the legacy of Lord Shelburne's lackey, and self-declared hater of our young United States, Adam Smith.

The error of Smith and his like, in particular, was not merely a mistake; it was, and remains, a malicious quality of error of conception, a misconception premised on the doctrine of the notorious Venetian scoundrel and founder of modern Anglo-Dutch Liberalism, Paolo Sarpi. Adam Smith stated his case for Sarpi's policy most precisely, in his 1759 *Theory of Moral Sentiments*. After the inherent folly of contemporary Keynesians and their like, is taken into account, there is nothing notable in their productions which was not already implicit, as confessed Adam Smith dupe Karl Marx insisted on this, in the argument presented, axiomatically, in the relevant summary presented as an often cited, crucial, single paragraph in that *Theory of Moral Sentiments*.

The incompetent, but nonetheless prevalent teachings of the modern Liberals on the subject of economy, such as those of the Physiocrats who followed the *Tableau Economique* of Deer Park *habitué* François Quesnay and the British Liberal school, as throughout much of a globally extended modern history since, are those teachings based, seemingly almost universally, on that rule set by Paolo Sarpi, as restated in raw terms by Smith in that and other locations.[6]

With rare exceptions, it would appear that virtually almost everyone had been lured, so far, into believing in a so-called "physical" doctrine of what is, actually, a form of mere mathematics, a doctrine which is universally absurd, or worse, in the effects of its practice. That folly is to be recognized in a notion which is believed, because it is heard that it is to be believed by any who do not wish to be ostracized from the profession; such is the notion that prevails among a certain class of worshipful dupes who wish to be delivered personal benefits from the hand of predatory authorities in high places. So, it had become the custom of most economists, and their dupes, to tell one another the lie, over and over again, the lie that the proper rules of economy are mathematical-statistical in nature.

In Summary of This Introduction:

The properly decent role of money, is not that of defining "economic value," but as a medium of assigning uttered credit estimated at a fair approximation of anticipated net physical cost,[7] in preliminary guess-work, not actual value. This notion of a political assignment

5. The Laxenberg, Austria-based International Institute for Applied Systems Analysis, which was spun off from the Bertrand Russell circles in the Cambridge school of systems analysis. Even positivists such as Germany's David Hilbert could not stomach such Russell-spawned wretches as those of the Russell cult of Professor Norbert Wiener and John von Neumann.

6. Considerable effort has been expended in efforts to hide the sheer "kookishness" of the notorious Deer Park's familiar Quesnay. Quesnay did, indeed, describe some of that structure of the French economy which echoed the creation of a modern French economy under Jean-Baptiste Colbert, but Quesnay's rationale itself was an apotheosis of kookery, attributing the productive powers of labor to the magical powers inhering in the awarding of the title of nobility to the estate's proprietor.

7. Including a charge, over incurred direct cost, for sustaining a justified rate of margin for progress of the physical economy as a whole.

of credit was introduced to the world in the guise of a notion from the mid-Sixteenth Century Massachusetts Bay Colony under the direction of Winthrop and the Mathers, that during a period prior to the British nullification of the Colony's charter.

This conception of credit, which has been more or less unique to the intent of the United States' Federal Constitution since that time, whenever that law has been observed in practice, has been an essential distinction of the constitutional superiority of the American System of political-economy over the intrinsically imperialistic, monetarist systems of those nations of Europe which have operated under that recent influence of the British empire which has been expressed, especially, by the British monarchy's rapacious Inter-Alpha Group, since 1971, up through the present day.

Unfortunately, not only our own United States, but the world at large, is presently held in the grip of a deep plunge of the entire planet's physical economy into a general breakdown-crisis which emerged in that apparent form inside the United States itself, during the late Summer of 2007. This disaster was made possible by nothing more significant than widespread belief in what is taught to the credulous as economics, in schools, universities, and the popular press, still today.

Under the present trends, the trans-Atlantic economies, which are already plunging into what is not merely a terrible depression, but an actual breakdown-crisis comparable to that of Europe in the latter half of the Fourteenth Century, are doomed if present trends in policies are permitted to continue. Although the major nations at the Asian borders of the Pacific and Indian Ocean have a far saner policy, such as that of promoting nuclear power, rather than the radically low-energy-flux-density practices of those foolish representatives of the rapidly collapsing trans-Atlantic group, even the nuclear-power advocates among those nations lack the strength to resist the effects of any continuation of the presently accelerating breakdown-crisis operating in the trans-Atlantic region.

Without the scrapping of that Liberal form of economic policy typified by Adam Smith, there is no present hope for avoiding a rapidly accelerating plunge of the entire planet into a generations-long, planet-wide, New Dark Age for all humanity.

Therefore, the subject of this present report, is the set of principles required for guiding the needed change in choice of economic policy-making principles, a transformation from the presently failed, British-dominated, world monetarist system, to the credit-system of a physical economy in accord with the principles underlying the U.S. Declaration of Independence and the initial terms of the U.S. Federal Constitution.

I. The Science of Physical Economy

To introduce the reader to the core of the principles of a science of physical economy, consider the following.

Since the beginning of the Twentieth Century, the proper modern understanding of the physical principles which underlie a competent science of physical economy, has been most clearly expressed in terms of that development of a *specifically human* practice of *physical chemistry*,[8] as by such as, most notably, both Chicago's William Draper Harkins, and, in a more elaborated form, as premised on Academician V.I. Vernadsky's scientifically crucial elaboration of the notion of mankind's efficient role as a species in *an anti-entropically developing universe*. The latter development, that of Vernadsky, expresses the essential characteristic of a universe which subsumes the three subspatial domains of the *lithosphere*, *biosphere*, and *noösphere*.

This experimental knowledge is premised upon the revolution in a science of physical chemistry which was introduced as being among the most crucial of the products of the influence of Bernhard Riemann's 1854 habilitation dissertation. This view has supplied the basis for relevant, essential discoveries of physical principle by such already noted, exemplary figures typified above by such names which I have already referenced repeatedly here, those of Max Planck, William Draper Harkins, V.I. Vernadsky, and Albert Einstein.[9] The best expression of that domain within which, and upon which the human creative powers act, is the notion of a universe defined by Einstein as Johannes Kepler's "finite, but unbounded universe," a definition, which, when considered today, includes the superior universality of an enveloping universal domain of *cosmic radiation*.

---

8. N.B. The *practice* of physical chemistry is specifically unique to human behavior—e.g., as by V.I. Vernadsky, and does not exist in the known universe otherwise.

9. Notably, this list excludes the functionally corrupt schemes of those empiricists or positivists who are sometimes mistakenly included in such a list.

The completed picture of that science of physical economy, pertains to the characteristics of the intrinsically noëtic function of those sovereign, creative powers of the human intellect which supersede the more ordinary functions commonly associated with the human brain, functions of that higher form of existence, better identified as "the work of the human mind, rather than the mere brain," functions which, we should emphasize as being expressions of a willful quality of distinction, a distinction which sets the human species, with its noösphere, absolutely apart from, and above all other known species of the lithosphere and biosphere.[10]

Those, just listed, absolute, categorical distinctions of man from higher ape, define man as evidently supreme among known expressions of a universe which is that of what Einstein defined as Kepler's "finite, but unbounded" universe, a universe which is, already, itself, essentially noëtic overall. Any competent use of the term "humanism," pertains to the implications of this set of sundry considerations.

I repeat, for necessary emphasis: any competent approach to a subject of economy, is premised upon these foregoing considerations. These considerations are, in turn, subsumed by the relevant dynamics of the social relations among the persons composing society, as Gottfried Leibniz supplied a modern definition of the ancient concept of *dynamis*, or, in modern terms, Leibnizian *dynamics,* as this is also indicated, implicitly, in the conclusions respecting social behavior set forth in the concluding paragraphs of Percy Bysshe Shelley's *A Defence of Poetry.*[11]

The lattice-like structure of the Eiffel Tower poses the issue of optimization of construction, "in a physical space-time defined in terms of the chronology of physical chemistry."

The characteristic feature of socially relevant human behavior, is the development of human society through what are *ontologically noëtic* changes in individually motivated "mass behavior," as Shelley implicitly defines such a principle of human behavior in the concluding paragraphs of his *A Defence of Poetry*.

These considerations, then present us with two issues as interdependent: **1.)** That the universe is creative, in and of itself; **2.)** That the inclusion of mankind in that universe, as being a consciously creative thinker and actor, provides the additional, unique factor of known *willful choice* lacking in other living species, the creative factor of what are to be distinguished as the specifically creative aspects of the human individual will, as *subsuming the actual development* of what may be otherwise defined as that universe. It is a quality which the existence of a developing set of individuals

---

10. The distinction of the human mind from the human brain, touches the principled distinction of a process of discontinuities, from one of particles. Admittedly, such distinctions do not exist in the opinions of those who have been drilled in the Liberalism of the followers of Paolo Sarpi; rather, such distinctions belong to the domain of *dynamics*, as the latter term was defined, originally and still uniquely to the present day, by Gottfried Leibniz as being an echo of the Classical "Greek" principle of *dynamis*.

11. The popular use of the term "dynamics," which implies a percussive effect, in incompetent use for music, and otherwise, must be put aside, as intrinsically absurd, and as an effort to suppress the definition supplied earlier by Leibniz. Notably, the shift of the reading of the periodic table of Mendeleyev and his followers from the choice of the element or isotope as an object of reference within the updated "table," from the implied notion of the particle, to the singularity of a domain of cosmic radiation, is now the great leap needed for the next step of prog-

ress in elaboration of the deeper implications of Mendeleyev's great work.

The exploration and colonization of Mars raise questions of fundamental science, notably involving the difference between the respective gravitational fields of the Earth, Mars, and the space between them, and the effect on the human crew of ploughing through the field of cosmic radiation en route. Shown is an artist's rendering of a Mars vehicle and the outposts of a Mars colony.

of humanity adds, uniquely, to change the universe as otherwise defined.

On that same point, the properly conceived, specifically human notion of a conflict between good and evil, is defined by considering the contrasting effects of the promotion or suppression of that benefit of human creativity which is typified, in effect, by the increase of the *applied energy-flux-density*, per capita and per square kilometer, as expressed in the increased physical productivity of societies, per capita, and per square kilometer of territory.

Thus, for example, we must address the case of that fraudulent doctrine for geometry which is attributed to Euclid, a set of dogma which, like the argument of the hoaxster Rene Descartes, denies the existence of the role of increases in the equivalents of "energy-flux density," denials such as the so-called "environmentalist" dogmas adopted in many places today. That fraudulent notion typifies the influence of what is properly regarded, for its effect, as a virtually "pro-Satanic" form of evil.[12]

Thus, the issue just proposed in that manner, has the

following, two interdependent aspects.

On the one side, we have **1.)** The effect of man's choice of increasing the equivalent of the energy-flux density represented by mankind's relevantly efficient forms of action upon the universe, and, **2.)** The form in which the interaction occurs between the individual mind and the social process in which the individual's action and related influence is situated.[13]

The relationship defined as the interaction between these latter two considerations, is of the manifold character of both the ancient term *dynamis* and Gottfried Leibniz's introduction of the comparable modern conception of *dynamics*, as Plato, in the **Parmenides**, in which he, for example, points out this type of notion which was adopted for modern physical science by Leibniz's famous attack on the thorough incompetence of the work of Rene Descartes and similar followers, such as the infamous Adam Smith's Ockhamite cult of modern Liberalism, *aka empiricism*, or, known otherwise as the cult of *positivism*, which was implicitly founded by the modern irrationalist Paolo Sarpi.

As Albert Einstein emphasized, in his appreciation of the genius of the great scientific discoverer of gravitation, Johannes Kepler, Kepler's universe is always

---

12. Notably, that Philo of Alexandria also known as an associate of the Christian Apostle Peter, condemned Aristotle for asserting a doctrine which implied that God had suddenly become permanently impotent once the act of Creation of the universe had been completed. It was from that Aristotelean presumption that the notorious Friedrich Nietzsche composed the slogan, "God is dead."

13. E.g., Plato's ridicule of the paradox of Parmenides. The Parmenides paradox is, notably, expressed by the intrinsic incompetence of all of the modern monetarists (e.g., the positivists).

finite, but never bounded, as this fact is consistent with the definition of *an inherently anti-entropic universe*. This means that both the abiotic domain, which is V.I. Vernadsky's *Lithosphere*, as also the *Biosphere*, and the *Noösphere*, are each and all inherently (anti-entropically) creative; but, only mankind's *Noösphere* is presently known as a *willfully* creative phase-spatial domain.

To illustrate a crucial point, take the following case to be taken as an example, from the attempted colonization of Mars.

For example, there are two cases in which the matter of the standard gravity experienced on the Earth's surface becomes a crucial practical issue for a mankind looking into our future existence within the Solar System. The *first*, is the difference between the gravitation to be experienced by mankind on earth and on the surface of Mars, and that, estimated at about one-third of that on the surface of Earth. The *second*, is the problem posed by considering the effect of what might be presumed to be the standard, nominally low gravitational field encountered in travel by human passengers through both Earth's surface and the field of cosmic radiation defined by the space traversed between Earth-orbit and the gravitation to be experienced on Mars' surface. This presumed, low "standard" gravitational field must be corrected for the presumably required approximation of an Earth-like gravitational field, if we are to consider travel by human passengers of the spacecraft.

So, the effect of cosmic radiation is presented for our attention when we consider the transport of human beings between departure and arrival in a Mars journey. We require synthesized intensities of the same biological effect as gravitation, which, in turn, suggests ploughing through the field of cosmic radiation associated with the alternate acceleration and deceleration required for conducting such a mode for interplanetary journey by human passengers and crew.

These exemplary cases are to be situated in the same general class of challenges represented by the relationship between the level of development of infrastructure in Earth-based economies, and the net value in performance of production of the means of human individual life on Earth. We must place the two cases, development of infrastructure for physical economy on Earth, and the "infrastructure" required for human travel between Earth and Mars under the common categorical heading of "infrastructure." Therefore, we must apply the case for Mars-Earth travel as an example of the role of infrastructure in defining the productive powers of labor on an Earth-based economy.

That illustration has the broader significance of illustrating the point, in that, in the light of the projectable, ultimate unsuitability of the Earth orbit as a place for what might be presumed to be an indefinitely continued human habitation, we must foresee the need for future mankind's alternative choices of places for continued human habitation. Since, the Solar system itself, will present threatened, kindred sources of difficulty in a distant future time, we must project the destiny of distantly future, successive generations of mankind accordingly.

As I have used illustrations, previously, as aids to insight into the principled nature of such foreseeable challenges, we must adopt a certain kind of moral perspective for the span of future mankind, henceforth. Essentially, this converges on the challenge of defining future "synthetic" environments within which mankind could live happily, despite the unsuitability of the "natural environment" of a certain planet's raw system otherwise.

This, of course, demands an increase, by increasing orders of magnitude, of the *energy-flux density* of society's practice, per capita, far, far beyond those presently at our disposal. We might say, that the work of Academician V.I. Vernadsky brings us to what a future mankind should experience as the sense of a preliminary, relatively primitive kind of advance in scientific knowledge and practice which must be admired today, as a forerunner of the kind of processing of accelerating development of the relative power of mankind, far, far beyond anything presently imagined. We must, therefore, improve our manageable scientific imagination of what those future powers of mankind must become, and, thence, discover what actually does, or does not exist as optimal remedies for the problems posed by our desires, as a species, for improvements within our future universe.

The first among the next steps in that direction will include the future of a return of musical practice to the standard of anti-Romantic, Classical composition from the range of Handel, J.S. Bach, Mozart, Beethoven, Schubert, and Schumann, through such as Brahms. This must be done out of respect for the fact that it is the Classical principle of composition of poetry, music, drama, sculpture, and portraiture, which expresses and nourishes those creative mental powers, including discoveries of principle in the practice of physical science, from the domain of the imagination of the beautiful, the discoveries which are ruined by the habits of such wretchedness as the Romantics and modernists, and the ruin of physical science by the morally dead minds of the deductive/inductive mathematicians of the empiricists and their positivist schools.

The great issue of all aspects of science, including economy is the fact of the general ignorance, even among nominal scientists, of the existence of a universal principle which is named variously as anti-entropy, or "creativity," as appropriate for the domains of the universe generally, for all expressions of actually living processes, and the characteristic of all viable expressions of human cultures. Nonetheless, both the principle of creativity, and the distinction of its practiced expressions remain virtually unknown conceptions, even among scientists today, not to speak of economists generally today.

Most among our contemporary economists, and virtually all practice of financial accounting remain utterly ignorant in this matter, ignorant of a universal principle of both science and Classical artistic composition on which the successfully continued existence of society depends today.

II. The Secret of Real Economy

Some would caution me, that anyone writing to present a matter of scientific or comparable principle, as I do here, should state his case without "knocking" the claims of his putative rivals. However, as in such cases of scientific work as, for example, medical practice, or economics, one must not suppress reference to dangerous diseases. Such are the requirements for the subject here at hand.

Contrary to that ancient, delphic creature, Aristotle, and equally contrary to the avowedly unprincipled empiricist (or positivist) dogmas of the modernist devotees of Paolo Sarpi, we must consider the entire universe known to mankind's experience as actually being inherently "creative" in principle, or, in technical terminology, *"anti-entropic."*

That means, that all species, whether life-forms or non-living, have come into existence as products of a universalizing process of *anti-entropy*; even what we usually consider as being the so-called inanimate species of existence, are dominated by the role of the force

of what is qualitatively anti-entropy, in shaping their own existence. With mankind's appearance among the creatures of our planet, something absolutely new had been added to the repertoire, that something, the principle of mankind, which might have been copied from the Mosaic first Chapter of **Genesis**: *a principle of creative willful choice of the power of mankind's power for upward progress, through those new creations made possible by the principled characteristics specific to the human species. This is the concomitant of adopting that view of this matter which supplies us access to knowledge of that intention which properly underlies the proper notion of human spiritual immortality.*

This idea expresses a specifically human characteristic, but is also, nonetheless, often a systemically rejected notion today; but, despite all that, it is a conception which presents us with the quality which is specific to mankind: *the willfully anti-entropic characteristic attributable as being unique to the human species. Such is the very essence of all of mankind's willful progress in the quality of the intentions and achievements of the human social experience.* Any relative lack of relevant truly universal, scientific principle, such as that lack which is typified by the reductionism of both the Aristoteleans and the positivists alike, typifies the source of that frequently monstrous incompetence which is often still guiding the economies, and also of most of the economists of the world still today.

That much said thus far, that purpose which lies behind this presentation of the concept of "The Secret Economy" which I make here, requires that we shift the basis of the discussion of this subject, up to a qualitatively higher order of conceptions: away from the prevalent folly of judging an attributed economic value to money, to reaching appropriate physical standards for judging the effect of the society's management of money itself.

Therefore, here, I have now switched our attention from economy defined by money, to a qualitatively higher order of conceptions, the physical conceptions which always determine the fate of nations in the longer span of developments. Those are physical conceptions, which are not visible to the mere senses, but are known from the vantage-point of the effects of what has been rarely understood among leaders of nations until now: *the effects of the distinctive, higher powers of the individual human mind.*

I now define that change from the sensory, to the sublime, in the following preliminary terms of "definitions" and the like.

What, Really, Is the Human Mind?

As Adam Smith effectively confessed the wickedness-in-fact of his system, by identifying it, as I note here, as according to the reading of his intentions, as in the most crucial passage within his 1759 *Theory of Moral Sentiments*, so, today, almost the entirety of present-day accountants, economists, and financial and business leaders, affirm their adherence to Smith's delusion. Presently, so far, only the rarest among today's specialists in economic affairs, show even a meager conception of the principled way in which real economies actually function. The results of our accountants and also most putative economists, are to be recognized in the presently onrushing, global economic breakdown-crisis now at full tilt.

Thus, the presently overwhelming majority of certifiable economists, like the intellectually crippled accounting profession itself, presents us with by-products of that same old, widespread delusion embedded in Smith's own lunatic dogma.

So, because of just that habit often traced to Adam Smith, and also the failures of Smith's Marxist followers, the economy of the world today has been on a decades-long course of changes which are directed, in net effect, toward the presently onrushing, greatest collapse in all modern history, of the world's financial and physical economy, alike. Consider the case of Adam Smith in this light.

While Adam Smith's work itself, was a fraud from top to bottom, Smith was, therefore, only perversely "sincere" in his presenting that specific kind of delusion shared among such among his dupes as both an Adam Smith fanatic Karl Marx and our own Wall Street ideologues today. That is to emphasize, what Smith himself wrote in a crucial passage of his 1759 *Theory of Moral Sentiments.*

To wit, we have the following passage:

"… Hunger, thirst, the passion which unites the two sexes, the love of pleasure, and the dread of pain, prompt us to apply [these desires] for their own sakes, and without any consideration of their tendency to those beneficent ends which the great Director of nature intended to produce by them."

Adam Smith, thus, presents us with what is, in fact, the widely accepted, but wickedly incompetent conception of "money," a folly which has been prevalent throughout the world affairs up to this present time.

The popular desire for money as such, or the equivalent, has been, thus, the kind of passion which attaches the typically suggestible, economics-ignorant devotees of Wall and Threadneedle Streets to the delusion that either the means called "money," or a notion of the kindred power to purchase and to consume, is the measure of the political system of values by which a nation, or nations, might be ruled presently. Hence, as history demonstrates: with most people, most of the time, the result is, that their tendency is, in effect, to impair the quality of judgment which might have otherwise made them fit to rule themselves.

Such a specific form of lack of judgment respecting the notion of "wealth," such as that of the dupes of Adam Smith, is more the cause of the moral and other disorientation of entire nations than anything else.

Such is the state of mental disarray shown by the supporters of President Barack Obama's promotion of mass-murderous health-care and related economic policies in the U.S. Congress presently; what might be allowed as the most generous characterization of those misguided creatures in that body, is that they might be considered at least temporarily as "clinically insane." The result of this is, that the more that they themselves are virtually owned by their belief in what is sometimes termed "the magic of the monied market-place;" the more destructive of society generally, which their conduct becomes, in respect to even the subject-matters of what are presumed to be even simple economic facts.

So, as the *New Testament* reported that the Christian Apostle Peter once denied a certain essential truth in fact. He did so in a way which should remind us of certain members of the U.S. Congress, and others, who are, unfortunately, not saints, but who, nevertheless, would simply deny the truth actually known to them, not only pending the moment the proverbial cock had crowed thrice, but through the presently darkening night of civilization.

Consider the case of the Seventeenth-century Massachusetts Bay Colony for as long as it was still free of a direct British dictatorship of its internal economic and associated affairs. Consider that Commonwealth's development and use of its own currency for credit.

This success was continued until the point in time that that practice was suppressed by the British tyrants who came in to ruin matters there. *A political system of currency is necessary, but, only, when it is used as a*

"Peter Denying Christ," Rembrandt van Rijn (1660). The Apostle Peter's actions, LaRouche writes, "should remind us of certain members of the U.S. Congress, and others, who are, unfortunately, not saints, but who, nevertheless, would simply deny the truth actually known to them, not only pending the moment the proverbial cock had crowed thrice, but through the presently darkening night of civilization."

system of credit, rather than being degraded, economically, into a system of assumed value.

I emphasize the qualitative difference between the presumed economic value often represented by mere money, and real value as expressed by physical economy. *Whereas, monetary systems pretend to measure the value of physical wealth by the notion of money, any competently designed economies today would assess the usefulness of a currency, by the standard provided by what are the intrinsically physical values which can be adduced, best, today, from the standpoint of such paragons of a truly anti-positivist physical chemistry, such as Dmitri Mendeleyev, Max Planck, William Draper Harkins, Academician V.I. Vernadsky, and Albert Einstein.*

The contemporary developments in the direction of reviewing Mendeleyev's principle for the periodic table from the relatively more advanced standpoint of a universal system of cosmic radiation, typify the approach which must be developed for a deeper insight into the principles of physical economy today.[14]

Consider some historical examples on background, beginning with the case of Charlemagne:

France's Charlemagne had defined the precedent for modern systems of economy. This was expressed in such forms as his great physical-economic census, his system of local national government in crucially significant regional capitals, and his development of his revolutionary systems of inland waterways.

Charlemagne's reforms served as the precedent for the development and role of the great internal systems of rivers and canals, which provided the crucial steps toward modern European economy and the application of the same reform within our United States. Those inland waterways prepared the leap toward the revolutionary U.S. trans-continental railway systems, first, inside the United States, and, in turn, the transcontinental rail systems of Eurasia.

Now, the prospect of the combined effect of magnetic-levitation mass-transport systems and rail, which will connect the principal continents of the world, would render most ocean transport of freight technologically obsolete, because the modern successor of ordinary internal rail transport will have rendered much of ocean freight-transport technologically, and, therefore, economically obsolete.

Changes such as those, illustrate a general principle which will be expressed in future development of certain nearby Solar-system locations, such as our Moon and Mars, when they will have come to be considered, sooner or later, as having come to be considered, later, as within the bounds of our presently still young, new century's plausible instances of work and habitation. Typical problems to be overcome for the purpose of human transport and dwelling in nearby Solar space—and, later, beyond, must look to such future develop-

14. Cf. Peter Martinson, *Towards a New Periodic Table of Cosmic Radiation*, **EIR**, Vol. 37, No. 16, April 23, 2010.

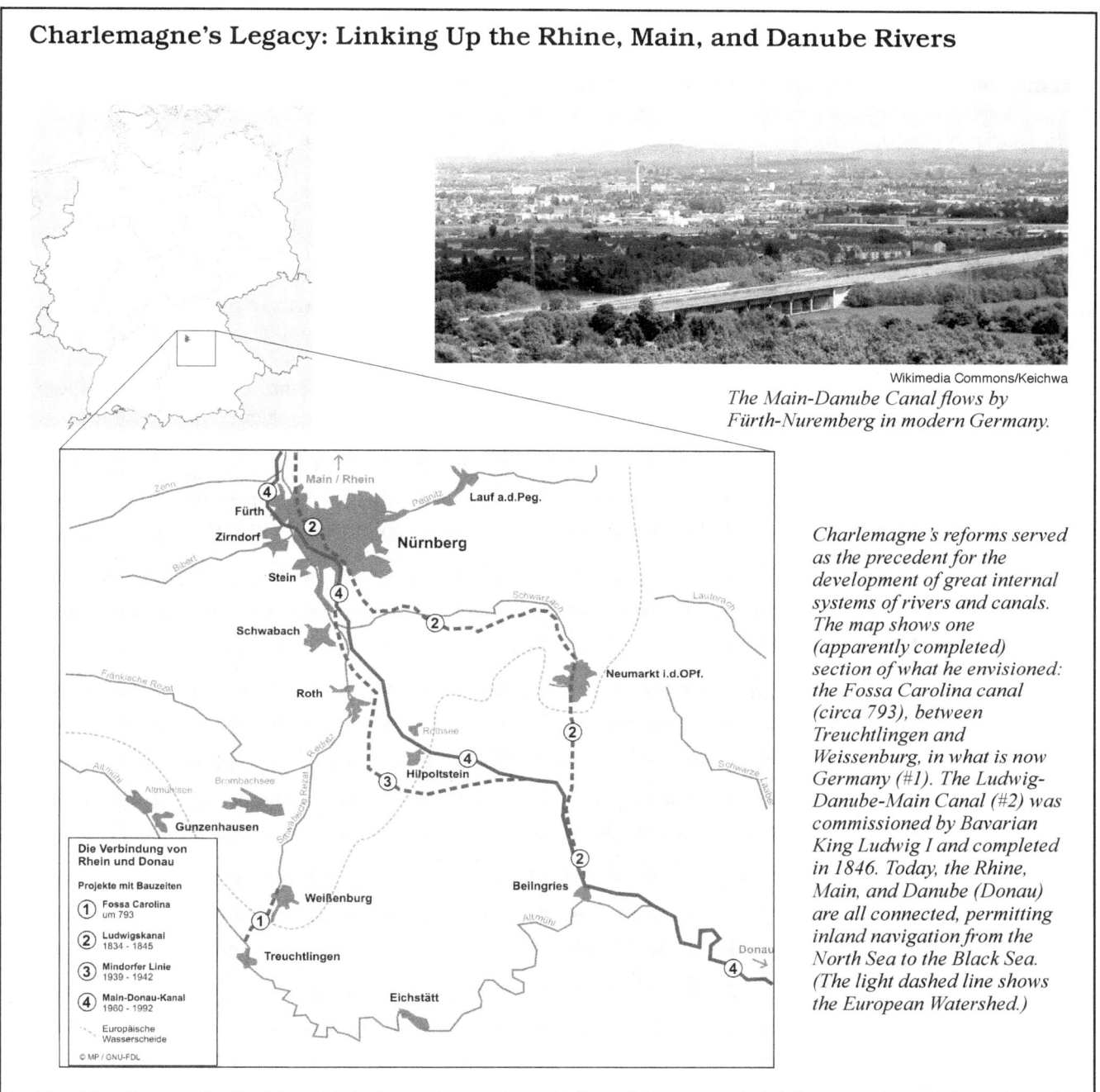

Charlemagne's Legacy: Linking Up the Rhine, Main, and Danube Rivers

Wikimedia Commons/Keichwa

The Main-Danube Canal flows by Fürth-Nuremberg in modern Germany.

Charlemagne's reforms served as the precedent for the development of great internal systems of rivers and canals. The map shows one (apparently completed) section of what he envisioned: the Fossa Carolina canal (circa 793), between Treuchtlingen and Weissenburg, in what is now Germany (#1). The Ludwig-Danube-Main Canal (#2) was commissioned by Bavarian King Ludwig I and completed in 1846. Today, the Rhine, Main, and Danube (Donau) are all connected, permitting inland navigation from the North Sea to the Black Sea. (The light dashed line shows the European Watershed.)

Die Verbindung von Rhein und Donau

Projekte mit Bauzeiten

1 Fossa Carolina um 793
2 Ludwigskanal 1834 - 1845
3 Mindorfer Linie 1939 - 1942
4 Main-Donau-Kanal 1960 - 1992

Europäische Wasserscheide

© MP / GNU-FDL

ments already foreseeable for later in the present century; we should then recognize that the development of basic economic infrastructure had always been a needed creation of what is required as an "habitable" development of a "synthetic," rather than a presumably "natural" environment for the enhancement, or even the possibility of human life and practice at some time in the existence of our human species.

For example: look back to the approximately hun-dred-centuries' interval of the Earth's last great glaciation. While some part of the human population had remained mired in the habits of life of some fixed, relatively narrow regions free of glaciation, great transoceanic maritime cultures were also developed. The requirement of a stellar mapping for navigation for the existence of maritime cultures, gave us the stellar notion of the efficient existence of a functional form of an ontologically actual universe, as echoed by such residual artefacts as the great pyramid of Giza, and by the physical science of *Sphaerics* known to the so-called Platonic long cycle and to the Pythagorean predecessors of Plato.

So, similarly, the fact of man's ancient knowledge and evidence of use of a fireside, as "fire" has been a crucial proof of the existence of the ancient distinction of man from ape, and that of "humanism," since no later than the bestial-like depravity of the mythical Zeus's proclamation against such physical-science expressions of human progress as the power of nuclear fission and fusion. Man as a creator in the likeness of the great Creator, is expressed by humanity's creation of the "artificial environments" we sometimes call "infrastructure," on which both the progress, and even the merely continued existence of civilized society depends.

Evil is thus typified by the attempted denial of certain forms of required human progress, such as denial of those measures which define the higher powers of improved basic infrastructure. Always, such progress depends upon mankind's increased power through the effects of what may be generally defined as needed increases in the energy-flux-density of the resources of applied, human-controlled power, as has been the case beginning with the discovery of improved forms of fire, such as the mandatory standard of nuclear-fission and thermonuclear fusion today, together with the progress of astronomy in the direction of man's exploration and prospective colonization in our planet's nearby space.

So, as we develop the means for satisfaction of those production requirements on the Moon which are needed to prepare mankind's escape to other planets and star-systems of our galaxy, from the present, prison-like bounds of Earthly habitation, we must include the need to meet the challenge of lower-ranking fields of gravitation, and the challenge of acceleration-deceleration in interplanetary flight to, and residence on Mars. Thus, we must do for interplanetary Solar space, what the great ocean-going mariners of the last great period of glaciation did in discovering astronomy as a practiced science, together with what Charlemagne did for the development of inland economy in Europe, with what we did in our initial development of the territory of North America, what we did in launching the concepts of transcontinental railway transport in North America, and with what must now be done in our commitment to a virtually continuous global system of transport and related infrastructure, beginning with the development of the Bering Strait railway tunnel. Thence, we must

now go on to development of our Moon, and, thence, to conquer the mysteries of transport through the larger domain of cosmic radiation, as for transport to and from and habitation on Mars.

That much said in the course of this present chapter of the report thus far, I would consider us prepared to plunge directly into the proverbial meat of the goals which I am now in the process of setting before us in this report.

Economics & the Human Mind

In my response to two successive, concluding questions presented to me at the May 8th webcast, I touched upon the most crucial of the underlying principles governing the successful functioning of the higher orders of the human mind. What I reported there, then, did not yet cover the fuller range of what has continued to be virtually unknown territory for most people, even most well-educated ones. However, what I stated on that subject on that occasion, did touch on the outlines of principles underlying the successful employment of the creative powers of knowledge of the human mind.

The reader's point of departure from this point as it will be considered in the next chapter of this present report, onwards, should also be a reference to the celebrated, and often bitterly contested *Parmenides* dialogue of Plato. For that reason, the problem to be considered there, is, thus, best outlined as follows.

At first estimate, as I proceed there, the human individual's knowledge of the universe he, or she inhabits, including even his, or her own skin, depends upon what is identified as our system of sense-perceptions. Yet, when we might attempt to understand the universe around us, even that which sense-experience presents as within us, none of those species of sense-perceptions, if considered one-by-one, presents us with a provably accurate set of facts about the real world which we might believe that we inhabit. Yet, at first estimate, all that we might believe that we know from such an organization of experience itself, does not yet show us the truth or falsehood of that experience of particular choices among sense-perceptions as such.

Such is the root of the ignorance of all such followers of both Euclid and the Paolo Sarpi of the modern Liberalism of today's empiricists and positivists. All scientifically competent claims to knowledge must be sought in other ways.

The most useful demonstration of this point which

EIRNS/Fletcher James

The great Renaissance artist and architect Filippo Brunelleschi (depicted here in a bust in Florence) discovered the physical principle of the catenary as the means employed to construct the otherwise practically impossible cupola of Florence's Cathedral, the Santa Maria del Fiore (also shown).

EIRNS/Bonnie James

is to be found for modern society, is that presented by two famous students of the works of those founders of modern physical science known to us, first, as the Florentine "Golden Renaissance's" Filippo Brunelleschi who discovered the physical principle of the catenary as the means employed to construct the otherwise practically impossible cupola of Florence's **Santa Maria del Fiore**, and, second, the related, much broader discovery of the essential principle of all competent modern physical science, by Cardinal Nicholas of Cusa. Among Cusa's most notable followers, are included, both the Christopher Columbus who adopted Cusa's injunction to cross the oceans to discovered continents, and the Leonardo da Vinci who presented the function of the tractrix from the catenary-tractix relationship; but, the most crucial discovery since the work of Cusa, was the founding of all competent subsequent progress in physical science, by Johannes Kepler.

Two features of the process by which Kepler developed his uniquely original discovery of universal gravi-

tation, are chiefly to be considered on this account here. First, *the principle of the elliptical planetary orbits*; second, *the universal principle of gravitation*. The first of these two, is to be considered as the precedent which prepared the way for the latter discovery. All the essential discoveries of these principles which were reported in finely elaborated detail, and, in large degree presented in England, by Kepler's writings, before the hoaxster Isaac Newton had made his silly, and since shown, factually, to have been fraudulent claims in all principled matters of the subject of modern science.[15]

The crucial feature of Kepler's work to be emphasized at this moment, is that his uniquely original discovery of universal gravitation can be employed by us today, as showing how we are enabled to escape from

15. No actually factual proof of anything contrary to what I have just written on this matter has ever been presented, or proven in any way. There are only professors and other opportunists who have chosen to "sing bad tunes for their suppers." Unfortunately, such opportunists are abundant among academics still today. Despite them, historical facts of science remain facts.

that unlit dungeon of the human mind which many among us impose upon ourselves as the habit of reliance on mere sense-perception. It was through Kepler's ironical juxtaposition of the harmonic organization of the Solar system to the contrasted visual notion of an array of Solar planetary orbits, that he was enabled to solve the riddle for which he has been praised by Albert Einstein: Einstein's judgment of Kepler's work, that Kepler presents us with a universe which is always finite, but never bounded.

To come now quickly to the matter of the significance, for all modern science, of what I have just written here respecting Einstein's grasp of Kepler's genius in these matters, compare Kepler's uniquely original discovery of universal gravitation, by comparing Kepler's achievement with that of Dmitri Mendeleyev's definition of physical chemistry's conception of the organization of the periodic table of elements. Or, presently, with the recognition that we must go further, to follow the combined achievements of Mendeleyev and V.I. Vernadsky, and as also the related achievements of Einstein and other leading founders of modern forms of anti-reductionist physical chemistry.

As Kepler's discovery of the principle of the Solar system illustrates this point, it was Kepler's successful resolution of the otherwise inescapable contradiction of the visual and harmonic sense of the ordering of the composition of the Solar system, which exemplifies the freeing of the human mind from the prison-like boundaries of a system of separated individual types of sense-perceptions.

No human sense-organ, nor scientific instrument, presents us with a truthful representation of our experience of the universe. It is, rather, the conjunction of mutually contradictory kinds of sense-perception, both those given us at birth, and those supplied as scientific instruments, which leads us to the discovery of relatively universal experimental truths.

Not merely that. The great fallacy of customarily believed notions of economy today, is the popular delusion to the effect of the presumption that the value of the products of human endeavor could be reduced to such an intellectually and morally degraded sort of misrepresentation of social realities, a misrepresentation of the type which would tend to prompt us to presume that statistical monetary phenomena are a tolerable measure of relative economic value. On that account, Adam Smith's and today's "Gospel according to Saint Lucre" is truly a worship of filthy lucre, and even much worse

than that, as the history of so-called "money-economy" attests so richly. A moral standard of scientific, rather than monetary truth, is required, instead.

Such considerations as these just presented by me here, point to the crucial significance of Plato's *Parmenides* for the training of the competently developed scientific mind today. In brief: true science begins with the mastery of the contradictions inherent in what are otherwise inherently false, simple interpretations of what we know through raw sensual experience, one at a time.

Therefore, next, we must take into account the difference between what most people, mistakenly, believe that they know from the brain's relationship to sense-perception as such, as compared with the more advantageous, higher standpoint of the mind's superseding the "level" of sense-perceptual experience through reaching the standpoint of universal physical principles, such as that I have often pointed toward by references to Brunelleschi, Nicholas of Cusa, Kepler, Gottfried Leibniz, Bernhard Riemann, et al. The latter of the two contrasted vantage-points, sense-perception versus the superseding vantage-point, is that which I emphasized in the two concluding replies to questions referenced above.

III. Dynamis: Your Brain, Or Your Mind?[16]

It should be no news to any among you, that the great majority among presumably literate citizens of Europe and North America, still, today, in particular, associate the location of the individual's personal identity, mistakenly, within the domain of sense-certainty.

That notion is associated with what is often a pathological quality of belief in, alternately, the choice among variable money-prices of objects, or the object identified with a relative value measured in terms of some specific kinds of objects, or experiences. The problem with that fact is, that as long as that traditional notion of standard for behavior persists, nations and their populations remain far worse than poorly equipped to cope, emotionally, or otherwise, with the kind of already terrible, and worsening physical-economic situation in

16. Cf. Gottfried Leibniz, "Specimen Dynamicum," in *Gottfried Wilhelm Leibniz Philosophical Papers and Letters*, Leroy B. Loemker, ed. Kluwer, Dordrecht 1989.

which they live, under the wildly galloping, worsening world crisis of today.

The custom of associating values of widely assorted types with money-values, is the notable result.

The root of this kind of self-inflicted danger to the credulous believers in such money-systems, either as a society, or, of some class of the members of societies, is that they continue, stubbornly, to associate human identity of persons with the reductionist's notion of the human brain and the experiencing of its presumably associated sensory apparatus.

That kind of assumption is the prevalent, grave error in the presumption, on which the folly of what is still generally accepted as "axiomatic" notions of value, is premised. Such are the presumptions on which most of today's economists and popular opinion, alike, have still been premised, often to obviously disastrous effect.

This pattern has been the known case since the inland imperial systems of the ancient Middle East, up through the global maritime empires of modern time. With the shift to maritime systems centered in the Mediterranean, in particular, a new, maritime pattern has become dominant in the European and trans-Atlantic cultural experience, over the millennia since the Trojan and Peloponnesian wars, in the world at large today: the dominant influence has become those imperial maritime traditions centered, in origin, within imperial forms of maritime cultures, a sometimes kaleidoscopic-like evolution which has come to be centered, since Europe's "Thirty Years War," in the emergence of the British Empire, up through the present date these lines are written.

Against that background, consider the naivety of the credulous, respecting those historically relevant, proper, higher functions of the human mind which they have failed to learn to control; they remain unable even to recognize the existence of those usually obscured, but available means, by aid of which they might regain control over the crisis-ridden destinies of their nations, and of themselves. So, since the Trojan and Peloponnesian Wars, what has become the dominant role of what we call European civilization, has been the handiwork of empires which have ruled their world through orchestrating murderous wars and conflicts, such as the follies of Europe's Thirty Years War and Seven Years War, and two so-called "World Wars," and such as the utter folly of President Obama's Afghan War, and the prospective attack by a London-puppet Israel against Iran, all wars with kindred effects among the befuddled ranks of subject nations and peoples.

The irony of this historical situation has been, that both the brain and associated sensory apparatus which are expressed by the adoption of such systems of values, even the presumed relative values of human beings, are considered as being merely sense-objects in and of themselves.

For example, consider the history of Europe and the U.S.A. *since the death of U.S. President Franklin Roosevelt, whether the assessment, from time to time, has been that the U.S.A. appeared to be in a state of growth, or recession, the fact is, that when value is measured in the trends over this entire interval, the physical-economic level of the U.S. economy has been consistently in a continuing process of measurably long-term physical-economic decline!* Thus, for example, there has been a continuing net decline in the physical-economic basic economic infrastructure of the U.S.A. since approximately 1967-68, a decline, such as that under British Prime Minister Harold Wilson's two terms, as masked for the edification of the pitiably credulous by the fraudulent doctrine of "creative destruction" which has been taught to the silly by Joseph Schumpeter.

The crucial proof which should have warned economists that the presumption behind that still popular opinion about money, is an error, is to be recognized in the evidence, respecting the Leibnizian principle of dynamics, supplied by a set of cases from both physical scientific knowledge, and from the Classical artistic composition which such celebrated poets and composers as England's Percy Bysshe Shelley identify in the concluding part of Shelley's own *A Defence of Poetry*.

That is the same point made by Gottfried Leibniz, over the course of more than several crucial works uttered on this specific subject-matter during, chiefly, the 1690s, in the course of his defining the only rational meaning given by anyone, to the subject of the role of *dynamics* as presented by him in defining the actual principles of modern physical science.[17] The best choice of an illustration of the principle commonly expressed by these given cases, is Albert Einstein's characterization of Johannes Kepler's uniquely original discovery of the principle of gravitation, as in Kepler's *The Harmonies of the Worlds*.[18]

---

17. Ibid.
18. Notably, exhibiting the characteristics of a system which is, in re-

The issue which I have posed here in the opening remarks of this present chapter, is not the possibility of taking advantage of some trick to be learned in school, or, by some correspondence course, or a gain of influence in society through a series of U.S. "Dale Carnegie" sessions. To avoid yet another round of such follies as those which I have just referenced, the higher powers of the human mind which might be made the common prowess of human beings generally, must be recognized by aid of the special form of scientific argument which I shall now preface in the course of this present chapter.

The Gravity of a Kepler Discovery

That said, therefore, now come directly, from the immediately foregoing, introductory discussion in this chapter thus far, to the crucial, underlying question to be posed to all economists: *What remains of a valid discovery of a universal physical principle of the universe, at a time when the physical brain of the unique individual discoverer of that universal principle no longer exists within this contemporary universe?* To begin this chapter's exploration of that matter, turn to the example of Johannes Kepler's uniquely original discovery of the general principle of gravitation, treating this as a point of departure, from which the reader should be able to build up an understanding of the notion of the relevant principle of physical economy which this question poses.[19]

Begin that exploration, most appropriately, as a matter of background, with the implications of the discoveries by Kepler for all competent expressions of modern physical science, still today. Out of this examination of the facts of the matter, find the answer to the question: *What is the human mind, really?*

During the recent period of several earlier years, relevant fresh exploration of Johannes Kepler's discovery of the principle of universal gravitation, had been re-examined by our association in a more thoroughly rigorous fashion than is to be found elsewhere in the usually recommended, contemporary scientific literature on that subject today. That was accomplished during a several years span of rigorously scientific reports produced by, chiefly, two successive team-efforts, each covering a phase of the subject from the premises of our Round Hill "basement"-area.[20] The first stage of that discovery by Kepler, had led to defining the physical principle of "equal areas, equal times" governing the elliptical pathway of the orbits of Mars and Earth. That study prepared the way for the more challenging second task, in which the team defined the physical principle of general gravitation, step by step, exactly as Johannes Kepler had already succeeded in doing.

Among other benefits, this work on Kepler's own original discovery also showed, for example, why the erring reductionist Pierre-Simon Laplace had not only failed the course, but, worse, had ended up with his terribly embarrassing failure expressed by his being mired in his infamous "three-body" paradox.

Laplace's error on this account, had been his blundering, systemic failure to accept the already existing, unique solution represented by the already available scientific knowledge of Kepler's unique successes in the discovery of gravitation. That is the discovery by means of which Laplace might have avoided a great embarrassment to his reputation. Even still today, Kepler's proven discovery is not only unique, but has also been a solution in the continuing tradition of such founders of all competent modern science as Cardinal Nicholas of Cusa, respecting the foundations of modern physical science generally. Study of this case of the failure of Laplace, helps us to understand more clearly the political reasons why Kepler's discovery of gravitation presented in Kepler's *Harmonies*, is not grasped competently by the positivist tradition to the present day.[21]

Laplace's state of intellectual, ontological numbness, was no mere matter of an academic oversight. Laplace, like Abbé Antonio S. Conti earlier, or Jean le Rond d'Alembert, Voltaire, Leonhard Euler, and others of similar bent, such as Laplace's accomplice Augustin

---

spect to all its internal revolutions, akin to the funicular curve (catenary) on this account, *always universally* finite, but not externally bounded.

19. See my extended replies to the concluding two questions of the March 8, 2010 LPAC Webcast, for a relevant complement to the argument presented here.

20. Very few from among the Twentieth-century physical-science university graduates, even from among the ranks of leading academic specialists in physical science, have ever actually worked through that material in a competent way as my relevant associates' "basement team" had done. The case of an attempted, but caught-out counterfeiting of the basement team's work, is notable on this account.

21. There are still leading universities in the world today, in which the corrupting influence of a mis-education of leading professors of physical science, especially the positivist fanatics, still teach their students wildly reductionist gibberish on the subject of Kepler's great discoveries.

Cauchy,[22] was a fanatical follower of the radical cult of Paolo Sarpi's Ockhamite Liberalism, and a key figure in what emerged later as the promotion of the Nineteenth-century Liberals' cult of mathematical positivism. Whereas, competent modern physical and related science was generated by such pioneers as Brunelleschi, Nicholas of Cusa, Johannes Kepler, Pierre de Fermat, Leibniz, Jean Bernouilli, by the Ecole Polytechnique of Gaspard Monge and Sadi Carnot, and by Carl F. Gauss, and Bernhard Riemann.

As Albert Einstein emphasized, it had been Kepler's comprehensive discovery in *The Harmonies* which has provided the seminal foundation of competent physical scientific method since that work by Kepler, such as the uniquely original discovery of the calculus by Leibniz, and the development of the principles of elliptical systems by leading contemporaries of Carl Friedrich Gauss. It was such followers of Cusa and Kepler as Gottfried Leibniz, Abraham Kästner's pupil Carl F. Gauss, Lejeune Dirichlet, and, especially, Bernhard Riemann, who established those foundations of the modern science traced to such outcomes as those of the work of Max Planck, Albert Einstein, and the principal founders of modern physical chemistry, such as Dmitri Mendeleyev, William Draper Harkins, and Academician V.I. Vernadsky. It is that latter "school" in modern physical science which is prominent in any principal argument to be made on the principal subjects addressed directly, or implicitly, in the course of this present report.

That much said, now return to focus attention on the crucial methodological feature of Kepler's solution for the defining of the Solar multi-planetary system.

---

22. With the final military defeat of Napoleon Bonaparte, the military hero of France's defense against the occupying Habsburg coalition, had been "the author of victory" and candidate for President of France to supersede Napoleon, Lazare Carnot. Carnot was replaced, on orders from the British and Vienna Congress occupation authority of the Duke of Wellington. As a by-product of this set of actions by Wellington, the world's then leading scientific institution, the Ecole Polytechnique was taken over by British-sponsored agents Laplace and Cauchy, and the leaders of French science, Monge and Carnot were not only expelled, but the scientific training program was taken over and polluted by the occupying alien forces. As a result, the Alexander von Humboldt who had been a fellow-member of the Ecole with Lazare Carnot, came to science's rescue, by unleashing the effort to move the legacy of the original Ecole to Germany, during the late 1820s. Under this arrangement the patriots of the Ecole continued their work through cooperation with the international circles, including leading U.S.A. science circles themselves associated with such outstanding figures as Alexander Dallas Bache, and closely tied to Carl F. Gauss and Alexander von Humboldt.

The History of the Issue

The key to that discovery, as Kepler laid out the case in a thorough fashion within his *The Harmonies*, is Kepler's emphasis on the ironical, systemic conjunction of *two, contrasted human sense-organisms, sight and the harmonics of sound,* a conjunction which was the unique basis for the original discovery of universal gravitation as made, initially, by him.

It must be emphasized, that Kepler never, as some have alleged, repudiated, but only superseded the starting-point of his initial hypothesis respecting the Solar system's organization, in noting that the ordering of the planetary orbits with respect to the Sun strongly suggested the provisional hypothesis that the ordering corresponded to the series of the Platonic solids. Rather, he had discovered, in the course of his *The Harmonies*, that no single sense-organ could define the set of orbits, but only a systemic contrast of vision to the harmonical order of hearing. Kepler refined his reading of the Platonic ordering by his later discovery of a still higher physical principle which answered the question: "Why were the planetary system's orbits arranged in this way?"

To sum up the problem which this fact of the originality of Kepler's discovery poses for the contemporary reductionist fanatic among academics, as for others, the issue is, still today, the menacing combination of the succession of Kepler's two central discoveries respecting the organization of the Solar system. This role by Kepler, represents, still today, an implicitly fatal blow against the reputations of the two principal rival systems of world-outlook, the first, that of Aristotle (and his follower Euclid) and the second, that of the founder of modern empiricism and positivism alike, Paolo Sarpi. This is the Sarpi from whom all generally accepted, but utterly incompetent notions of principles of economy in use today have been derived, such as that of Adam Smith, of the Russian IIASA dupes of Bertrand Russell's school of Cambridge "systems analysis,"[23] and, of the positivist fanatics, who insert the numbness of their intellects into the idea of number.

The History of the Conflict

The history of the conflict between the followers of Brunelleschi and Cusa, on the one side of modern science, and the modern batches of empiricists and posi-

---

23. E.g., IIASA (the Laxenburg, Austria International Institute for Applied Systems Analysis).

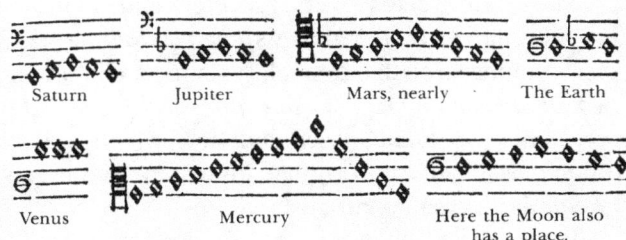

| Saturn | Jupiter | Mars, nearly | The Earth |

| Venus | Mercury | Here the Moon also has a place. |

Johannes Kepler.

Right: Geometrical model of the solar system as nested Platonic solids, from "Mysterium Cosmographicum." Above: Harmonic relations of the planets expressed in musical notation, from "The Harmony of the World."

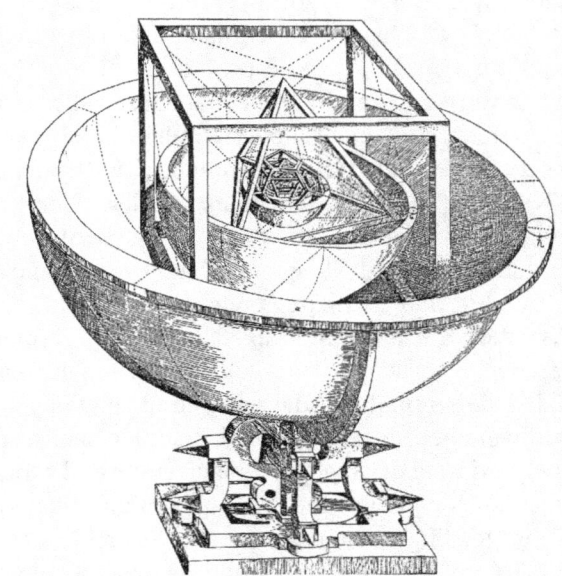

The key to Johannes Kepler's discovery of universal gravitation and the planetary orbits was his emphasis on the conjunction of two, contrasted human sense-organisms: sight and the harmonics of sound.

NASA

tivists collected under the banner of the image given to the actually silly, and fruity, but extremely unfruitful Sir Isaac Newton, is a reflection of that cultural revolution, known as modern Liberalism, led by Paolo Sarpi and his Leporello of pseudo-science, Galileo Galilei. Typical of the opposition to these hoaxsters of Sarpian Liberalism was the case of Pierre de Fermat, whose original discovery of the principled implication of refraction, had an additional, crucial outcome in the later collaboration of Gottfried Leibniz with Jean Bernouilli in developing the principle of universal least action.

The principal targets for initial attempts at destruction of existing science by the circles of Sarpi and Galileo, were the circles of Nicholas of Cusa and Cusa's follower, that great giant intellect among the followers of Cusa, Johannes Kepler. The setting of this attack is located in the coincidence of the span of the births and deaths of Kepler (1571-1630) and Sarpi's virtual "Leporello," Galileo (1564-1642), respectively. Not only were the two cases historically parallel, but Galileo's relationship to Kepler was that of spying against him in Sarpi's interest, using Kepler's active correspondence, on the subject of music, with Galileo's father Vincenzo, a coincidence which afforded a spying Galileo Galilei the opportunity to spy on Kepler for the purpose of launching an attack intended to contribute to discrediting him by aid of frauds perpetrated against Kepler's scientific achievements, as this was done by Galileo himself in his capacity as an leading agent of Paolo Sarpi.

The larger significance of these developments is rarely understood, even among relevant professionals today. In point of fact, the issues were posed, on the one side by the great Renaissance scientific revolution launched, most notably, by Brunelleschi and Cusa, and by Cusa's followers, and, on the opposing side, was the modernist Liberalism of Paolo Sarpi. Isaac Newton was, essentially, merely a concocted, pseudo-scientific hoax created in the interest of the Liberalism of Sarpi and his lackey Galileo. The connection was that maintained through the adoption of Galileo follower and fanatical Cartesian, the Abbé Antonio S. Conti notorious for the creation of the ill-deserved scientific reputations his own lackeys, such as Isaac Newton and the hoaxster and Leibniz-hater Voltaire.

We shall return to the subject of Kepler's significance for the study of the deeper principles of the human mind, in the next chapter of this present report.

The Root of Modern Political Economy

Now, proceed to re-examine the definition of the actual human mind from the standpoint of the most relevant aspects of physical science, especially a physical science of economy. The following, interpolated information, on background, is essential for providing the setting of the argument to be made respecting what may be titled "A View of the Real Human Mind In the Real World of Today."

In any well-known history of a European civilization's new attempts at science since the death of Plato, the notion of science is to be recognized as centered on a conflict among three mutually exclusive alternatives in choice of underlying, presumed universal physical principles, as follows.

The first member of this designated series, taken from that relative antiquity, is the Delphic cult of Aristotle; the second, in opposition to the Aristoteleans, is best identified as represented by the work of the Florentine Renaissance of Filippo Brunelleschi and Nicholas of Cusa; whereas the third, is that of the irrationalist school of Paolo Sarpi and of the set of his radically reductionist, nominally empiricist or positivist followers. The mutual differences among these three categories, are not matters of approximation; they are essentially systemic.

Nevertheless, it is to be both noted and emphasized, that Brunelleschi and Cusa, taken as representing successors in working through the development of a single experimental conception, represented an escape from the decadence of, in particular, what had long been the Aristotelean school, to return to not only a return to the most advanced scientific outlook of the pre-Aristotelean science of the Pythagoreans and their like, such as that of Plato, but, also, to bring on a qualitative advance in respect of underlying principles of physical science which went beyond the noble achievements of some of the pre-Aristotelean thinkers.

The crucial, common point of distinction of both the work of Brunelleschi and that of Cusa, had been the coincidence of their discovery of the essential content of modern European science, which was the discovery, initially by Brunelleschi, of the use of the principle of what would come to be understood as the catenary (or, "funicula"), as a critical principle of feasibility in construction, a discovery by Brunelleschi whose fulsome recognition would be specific, later, to the combined achievements of Gottfried Leibniz and his collaborator Jean Bernouilli. For our purposes at this immediate point in this report, it is sufficient to enter the following note on the subject of the catenary, the principle on which Brunelleschi depended for the feasibility of the construction of the cupola.

The catenary is to be recognized as *a physical curve*, as distinct from the ordinary, a-prioristic reading of the curves known to Aristotle or Euclid, or the relevant failure of Sarpi's advocate Galileo.[24] The earlier mystery, prior to the work of Leibniz, as associated with the attempts to define what came to be known as the catenary, was itself an essential by-product of the incompetence of the influence of the *a-prioristic* presumption of such as Aristotle and the Euclideans, the presumption that geometric forms, therefore, should be defined as an expression of a form extended to "infinity."[25] Gottfried Leibniz, working in the beginning of the Eighteenth Century, introduced a crucial difference, to the effect that the catenary belongs to *a physically finite, but unbounded* domain of action. Hence, the origins and the authority of the Leibniz-Bernouilli principle of least action.

Although that distinction was unique to Leibniz and his immediate associates, especially the associate Jean Bernouilli, the yearning for the same principle had been expressed already in the work of both Brunelleschi's design of the cupola for Florence's **Santa Maria del Fiore**, and in Cusa's principal scientific works beginning with his *De Docta Ignorantia*. The discovery of the physical principle which was also expressed by the catenary, was not the only relevant feature of the great impact of the successive achievements of Brunelleschi and Cusa at that time; rather, that principle typified the world-outlook spread by such as Brunelleschi and Cusa, that as reflection of the setting of the work of the great ecumenical Council of Florence. This set of conceptual foundations for both modern science and for the design of the economy of the modern form of sovereign nation-state, was spread from Cusa, explicitly, through such as France's Louis XI, England's Henry VII, and Christopher Columbus, and through such followers of Cusa as Leonardo da Vinci and Leonardo follower Niccolo Machiavelli.

The combined effects of the works of science and related statecraft of Brunelleschi and of Nicholas of Cusa, expressed the inclusion of principles of organization in statecraft which had never existed within post-Plato European civilization earlier. The effect of the revolutionary change expressed, chiefly, by the impact of the work of Cusa, produced a specific kind of effect which is best symptomized by the innovations in military and related statecraft featured in the writings of the follower of Cusa's follower Leonardo da Vinci, and the participant in the defense of the sovereign republic of Florence, Niccolo Machiavelli.[26] This revolution in statecraft which found its concentrated expression in the work of Machiavelli, stood as a great strategic rock against which the reactionary forces of the Habsburg tyranny had wrecked themselves in the course of the storms of religious warfare of the persistently recurring, 1492-1648 orgy of religious and related warfare.

The results of this had included the catastrophic failure of the Council of Trent. That failure, which was, in effect, chiefly the failure of the older ("Aristotelean") party of imperial Venice. a failure expressed as the practical political-strategic outcome of the Council of Trent. This was the failure which cleared the pathway for the rise of the new design of Satanic forces from within that oligarchical party of Venice then led by Paolo Sarpi. The popular name for that evil, New Venetian Party, still today, is the Anglo-Dutch variety of Liberalism presently typified by the British empire of today, that currently under the typical guise of the Queen's banker Lord Jacob Rothschild, et al., as typified by the implicitly bankrupt, presently hyper-inflated Inter-Alpha Group.

There are, of course, original features in the development of that British Empire of today, but, at the same time, that British Empire is only a new variant among a series of imperialisms defined as a product of the same system of a maritime cultural form of originally Delphic, Mediterranean-centered imperialism which emerged from the ruin of ancient Greece in the Peloponnesian War.

With the birth of what became the British Empire, as through the course of the British East India Company's triumph through its organization of the leading nations of continental Europe into a "Seven Years War," every effort to free the peoples of Europe from that recurring continuation of the British Empire, has failed until now, despite what proved to be the temporary defeat of the British Empire by President Franklin D. Roosevelt's United States. Roosevelt's successor, Churchill-steered and Wall Street-controlled President Harry S Truman,

---

24. The fraudulent, and utterly failed attempt to identify the catenary by devotee of Paolo Sarpi, Galileo, is notable as an exhibition of the systemic incompetence of the methods of the modern empiricists. All of my own early insights into physical science date from a relevant set of experiences at the age of 14-15. Thereafter, I always regarded Euclidean geometry as being intrinsically incompetent on these premises.

25. Galileo's claim to have discovered the secret of the catenary was simply a fraud.

26. Leonardo not only understood the catenary, as Galileo never succeeded in this, but defined the catenary-tractix function.

like Andrew Jackson earlier, betrayed the United States to the cause of British imperialism. The British empire made concessions to the American principle for the purpose of retaining its power during difficult times, but, since the successful assassination of the obstacle to British imperial power known as President John F. Kennedy, the British Empire has, in fact, dominated the world as a true imperial power from about February 1968 until the present date.

Only poor dupes, on the way to becoming slaves, believe in the mere fiction of a "U.S. imperialism" today. "Wall Street," the only evidence which might be claimed as evidence of a "U.S. imperialism," was never, since 1763, other than a British imperial parasite sucking the juices of Manhattan, as also many other locations from around this planet, all on British imperialism's behalf. Usually, those who argue that the U.S.A. is imperialist, turn out, on closer scrutiny to be branches of Threadneedle Street themselves, or, simply dupes of the tradition of the Karl Marx who had worshipped Adam Smith almost as a pagan god.

The Empire, Slavery & the Mind

The victors among the warring tribes of Africa often sold the selected, surviving portion of their defeated rivals into slavery. The surviving portion of the modern victims of this Africa practice's captives was transported, on the initiative of the victors in those internal wars of Africa, to the coasts of Africa, where the captives were sold to such as the Spanish, Portuguese, Dutch and British traffic in slaves, an enslavement which had begun with the delivery to port-areas of those Africans who had been enslaved by other Africans, and then delivered to the coastal ports founded by European slave-traffickers, ports whence the surviving assortment of captives was transported, still as slaves, to such destinations as the Atlantic coasts of the Americas.

Thus, the fact that the enslaved victims of this process had been brought into slavery to the Anglo-Dutch, Spanish, and Portuguese by Africans, does not diminish the degree of criminality of those Habsburg and related oligarchical interests who shipped the victims to a condition of enslavement in the Americas, much of this being done for the profit of the Anglo-Dutch, British Empire which controlled this Atlantic trafficking in slaves which had been conducted by the lesser oligarchs of Britain's system of imperial reign over the Nineteenth Century Spanish and Portuguese monarchies.

It should not be seen as our purpose here to account for much more than the following essential fact of that matter of the origins of the slavery within North America prior to President Lincoln's victory.

The growing Americas market in such trans-Atlantic traffic in African slaves, was prompted largely by the fact that the indigenous tribes of the Americas were usually ill-suited for use as a slave-class in the Americas. The significance of the African slave was that he had been a product of the dynamics of a systemic form of customary practice of the violence of enslavement within relevant parts of Africa itself.

This was the influence under which African slaves temporarily adapted to submission to slavery in an Americas where the African had no roots, where the indigenous American tribes, such as the case of the literate culture of the pre-Andrew Jackson, Cherokee nation, were not as well suited for a system of slavery. The process of the subsequent liberation of the slaves in our U.S.A., the liberation from the British empire's authority over the continuing Spanish and Portuguese traffic into slavery within our republic, was, therefore, shaped largely by a powerful lurch toward personal freedom within our own republic itself, a struggle of various sorts, but one rooted in the emergence of the American cultural climate of intellectual freeing of the former slave. It was the slave's desire for children of marriage, combined with the indispensable role of President Abraham Lincoln's dedication to a victorious war against Lord Palmerston's British imperialism for defense of the U.S. republic, which secured the indispensable freeing of the slaves in the only way it could have occurred, as Frederick Douglass understood, violently, that by the action of our Federal Republic against the British system of trans-Atlantic slavery.

The principle which I have invoked in presenting this example from the history of mankind's effort for freedom from enslavement of man by man, is to be found on a still deeper level, in the principle named *dynamics* (e.g., *dynamis*) by Gottfried Leibniz, or what is the same principle of dynamics illustrated in the concluding summary in Percy Bysshe Shelley's *A Defence of Poetry*.

This return to the subject of *dynamics* now brings our attention back to our principal subject in this report, the distinction of the higher functions of the human mind from the undeniably indispensable, but qualitatively inferior functions of the human brain.

IV. The Empire & Your Mind

It is sufficient, and also justified, that we should tend to limit the scope of this present report to the examples of the essential, clinical facts bearing on the history of the birth and evolution of what can be efficiently classed as a Mediterranean-rooted European civilization, as known since both the fall of Babylon and the rise and decline of the Persian Empire. However, we can not overlook certain essential features of the development of a Mediterranean offshoot of an Atlantic maritime culture which rose to power out of the misty past of the Mediterranean empire, nor should we overlook certain up-river developments, such as those of the Nile, within the territory of what was to become either a European culture, or nearby-Asia cultures which were established, largely, by what are appropriately identified as "the Peoples of the Sea." We must include the cases of the Nile, Mesopotamia, the Indian Ocean, and the Black Sea offshoots, such as the Hittites of Anatolia, and of maritime cultures, such as that of the Sumer which was initiated by "Peoples of the Sea," that during no less than the several millennia preceding Homer's Trojan War.

What has emerged out of the background of maritime cultures from a succession of several millennia preceding the Peloponnesian War, has been the legacy of the domination of an emerging Mediterranean-centered civilization out of an ancient oligarchical system of actual, or virtual slavery, or "serfdom." This was a system whose essential features had been consistent with that myth of the Olympian Zeus, a myth which is to be associated with the hierarchical form of oligarchical tyranny depicted by Aeschylus' **Prometheus Trilogy**, a record which is not inconsistent with the images evoked for the scholar by the relevant chronicles of Diodorus Siculus.

My own approach to the study of the principles of the human mind, has brought some among us to a view, here, of that history, a view which I identified within a preliminary outline of the matter in the course of the preceding chapter, and which I now examine more critically in the present one.

The most characteristic, and defining fact about human cultures, as distinct from those of those types of lower than human forms of life which include the mammals generally, is that the human genotype is potentially, consciously, and uniquely *creative* in a sense of those matters which are consistent with the scientific-technological factors of a qualitative, willful succession of changes in the willful behavior of our species itself, a quality of change which is lacking in all other, known species, including those of animal life generally. For example: consider the crucial fact of the uniqueness of mankind's willful use of fire. Or, consider the uniquely original discovery of the principle of gravitation by Johannes Kepler, as Kepler's work was clarified by Albert Einstein on this account, as a "water-tight" choice of relevant example of this distinction.

In the use of the term "creative" by me here, as this was referenced at some length within the preceding chapter, I mean the power of the human species to bring about *willfully ordered*, qualitative increases in the potential relative population-density of the human species, as no other known species of living creature has proven itself able to accomplish such intentional changes as those to be seen in the potential of our own species, as, for example, by even a single individual's single true discovery of a universal principle. The natural potential for the healthy development of an individual personality, is that which is so defined as being the implicit quality of a "demi-god," that in the particular sense of the quality assigned to man and woman by the opening chapter of **Genesis**.

However, at the same time, it is notable that common practice among known societies, has included the application of a general prohibition against the option for using such a creative power by any member of those so-called "lower social classes" who is not explicitly authorized, as if by a "laying on of priestly academic hands," to have access to the actual knowledge of even free use of such creative potentials. Thus, there has been the legendary, symbolic banning of the "use of fire" by the Olympian Zeus of the Prometheus trilogy, a ban which illustrates the dominant habit of practice of virtual slavery, or serfdom, imposed upon the greatest relative number of members of society, just as the "Babylonian-priesthoodlumism" of today's "environmentalist" cults, such as that which British Prince Philip's World Wildlife Fund prescribes as the urgently demanded practice of relative genocide, world-wide, today.

Against the background of those considerations which I have outlined immediately above, let us now

Shelley: 'A Defence of Poetry'

From the essay by Percy Bysshe Shelley (1792-1822):

[W]e live among such philosophers and poets as surpass beyond comparison any who have appeared since the last national struggle for civil and religious liberty. The most unfailing herald, companion, and follower of the awakening of a great people to work a beneficial change in opinion or institution, is poetry. At such periods, there is an accumulation of the power of communicating and receiving profound and impassioned conceptions respecting man and nature. The persons in whom this power resides, may often, as far as regards many portions of their nature, have little apparent correspondence with that spirit of good of which they are the ministers. But even whilst they deny and abjure, they are yet compelled to serve, the power which is seated upon the throne of their own soul. It is impossible to read the compositions of the most celebrated writers of the present day without being startled with the electric life which burns within their words. They measure the circumference and sound the depths of human nature with a comprehensive and all-penetrating spirit, and they are themselves perhaps the most sincerely astonished at its manifestations: for it is less their spirit than the spirit of the age. Poets are the hierophants of an unapprehended inspiration; the mirrors of the gigantic shadows which futurity casts upon the present; the words which express what they understand not; the trumpets which sing to battle, and feel not what they inspire; the influence which is moved not, but moves. Poets are the unacknowledged legislators of the world.

present the principal subject of this report, "the creative powers specific to mankind," under the title of the search for the true identity of what we might wish to identify as the ordinary quality of future "Promethean Man." I do not mean the childish fantasy of a "Superman," but, rather, what should come to be recognized as a specifically healthy mental type of creative intellectual capability of a type of ordinary human individual, an increased capability to be foreseen as emerging during the coming few generations, bringing us an ordinary man and woman of the type who is preparing, now, through self-development, for man's initial conquest of nearby Solar space by the time of the close of the presently young century.

The presently relevant evidence to that intended effect, is clear to me. Such an accomplishment is a feasible one within the range of what should be becoming typical of the closing decades of this present century. Keep that thought in mind, as we now proceed to develop the crucial point which I introduced briefly during part of the preceding chapter.

That said, turn back to the subject of the human mind at the point in the preceding chapter where I had left off: "What really is the human mind?"

That said, we return to the relevant point on the subject of creativity which we left off during the course of the preceding chapter.

The Real Human Mind

The problem I posed there, was the fact that the mental objects which we regard as sense-perceptions, are not a gallery of portraits of the real universe, but are more in the nature of shadows cast by that universe. As the case of Kepler's unique discovery of the principle of universal gravitation illustrates the problem to be considered; man's actual knowledge of the universe itself is limited to those kinds of crucial experimental proofs which treat the mutually contradictory experience of two or more respectively distinct sense-experimental experiences as clues to the actually functional object which had cast the relevant shadows of sense-perception.

This point in fact is made clearer through mankind's use of man-made instruments, such as microscopes and telescopes, as surrogates for sense-perception, instruments used as supplementary aids to access to experiences which the given human senses as such fall short of comprehending. In brief, we do not "see" the object which corresponds to sense-perceptual experience; we "see" what is experienced as a shadow cast by that which is the source of the experience. I repeat: what we actually "see," is not the experienced object, but a shadow cast on the mind by the presence of the actual object. What we must train ourselves to "see," is not what we tend to regard as an object in physical space-time, but, rather, the cause of a shadow which is cast upon the mind as the experienced reality: a *singularity*, rather than a "real object."

We must retrain our habits of thinking to enable us to conceptualize the "real object," to recognize it as the substance which is responsible for our experience of the mere shadow the naive observer had regarded, mistakenly, as an experienced "real" object of sense-perception.

So, in better-informed sorts of physics-language, we are enabled to experience the reality of a singularity in a field of "cosmic radiation." When we have trained our minds to do this successfully, our conscious mind enters an efficiently ontological state of awareness which is distinct from the realm of shadows which the naive mind treats, mistakenly, as if those shadows were a reality defined by mere sense-perceptions as such.

For example, consider the presently oncoming kind of change in experimental perspective with respect to the Mendeleyev periodic table. Nothing that we do in this way actually violates the evolved notion of the Mendeleyev view of the field; there is a degree of preserved correspondence between a periodic table emphasizing images of presumed material particles, and the "corrected" view, that of the singularities lying, primarily, within the universal domain of cosmic radiation. What we lose in making that change in point of mental view, is little more than what is now revealed to us as having been an habituated, relatively childish belief in the virtually tangible existence of "empty space."

In that fashion, our thoughts have now truly entered the domain of physical relativity. It is a step which seems to be only like putting a toe in the water, but the essential principle of the change in point of view is sufficiently clear, if lacking the sense of an experience comparable to that of actually swimming through the cosmic radiation which fills up what is mistaken for "empty" interplanetary space, that of future mankind sometimes traveling at relativistic speeds.

Lest some suspicious reader might suspect a bit of sleight-of-hand in all this which I have just presented here, think back to those ancient, ocean-going mariners who discovered a lawful unity, of a type useful for trans-oceanic navigation, in the area presented by the persistently changing night-time sky, by allowing for such changes as those associated with the long Platonic cycle, which came to the attention of such as a Bal Gangadhar Tilak's consideration of the Vedic calendar, as in his *Orion*.

There is no actually "empty space" in the actuality which naive observers may regard as the imagined space distinguishing the visible bodies attributed to the night-time sky from one another. For example: we must consider the role of magnetic fields as shown by certain singularities arising from the use of the equivalent of the compass in even what might be considered as pre-historic transoceanic navigation, as reflected in the known ancient cycles of the long-wave periodicity of the migrations of the North magnetic pole.[27]

The fact which I intend to emphasize in the course of these present remarks, is the effect of the change in conceptual standpoint, which I have just presented. Instead of treating the images associated with sense-perception as "the real world," we locate the experience of the real universe in the act of not only viewing sense-perception as presenting us with a shadow cast by reality; but, we must locate access to knowledge of reality in the person's consciousness of the fact that the sense-perceptual domain is merely a shadow cast by the real universe which he, or she actually inhabits. We do not actually "see" ourselves; but, rather, we see the experienced, projected shadow of that universe which we actually inhabit.

The viewpoint which I have just, thus, identified, should not be considered as a recently crafted novelty. If we translate what I have written here into a rather well-known fact of what should be recognized as a Classical regard for a knowledgeable experience of history, what I have just written here is no different in

---

27. For the sake of your powers of imagination, think back to the implications of a plausibly Phoenician, or comparable maritime culture's relic from trans-Atlantic navigation to be currently dated to as recent a time as from about four thousand years ago, to North Salem, New Hampshire, a site which my wife and I had examined, back in 1982.

substance than the ancient Classical Greek use of the term *dynamis*, or its modern expression as what Gottfried Leibniz named *dynamics*. As I have pointed out, repeatedly, this notion of *dynamics* is the same type of phenomenon which the poet Percy Bysshe Shelley presents as the phenomenon of changes in the characteristics of society's mass movements which he pointed out in the closing paragraphs of his *A Defence of Poetry*.

Shelley's point stated otherwise, is: "Reality haunts our conscience!" This prescient sense of the reality of *dynamis*, or *dynamics,* a domain which we actually inhabit, is most bluntly expressed in what is often regarded as a mysterious force of sudden surges of mass social phenomena, such as the present revolt of the conscience of the greater mass of our populations against the tyrannical obscenities superimposed by current governing powers upon the accelerated worsening of the conditions

The Washington National Opera

The power of creativity "on which a society's progress, and even survival, depends, is expressed most clearly in what can be identified as Classical forms of artistic composition," LaRouche writes. Here, The Washington National Opera performs Verdi's I Vespri Siciliani *in 2005. Maria Guleghina plays Elena and Franco Farina plays Arrigo*

of life of the vast majority of nations' populations. It also reflects those mental acts of what can be recognized as that genius of the greatest poets and scientists typically expressed as the ontologically distinct phenomenon of true metaphor, as the 1947 edition of William Empson's *Seven Types of Ambiguity* attempts to convey the notion of such a distinction of the sense of beauty to his readers, or as a true, but currently academically unpopular reading of Shakespeare, or of Friedrich Schiller, or the experience of Ludwig Beethoven's Opus 132, or Wolfgang Mozart's *Ave Verum Corpus*, relies on this aesthetical concept in an essential way.

'All the World's a Stage'!

The most accessibly rigorous demonstrations of this principle, include the putative "magic" of the finiteness of the Classical theatrical stage. There is evidence to this effect in the work of Shakespeare, but, for obvious reasons, Friedrich Schiller's work is a more accessible source of fuller means of available evidence supporting the relevant argument.

A proper notion of the concept of tragedy does not require real heroes presented on stage. As Schiller emphasized, the body of the principal actors presented as characters on stage does not require the attempted selection of heroes for the presentation of the drama. Shakespeare's *Julius Caesar*, *Lear*, *Macbeth*, and *Hamlet*, and Schiller's *Wallenstein*, are typical of a drama set within the actuality of a morally sick society, one without any true heros actually performing leading stage roles. As Schiller taught, the hero is to be sought in the member of the audience, like the children in Wallenstein, who is inspired to become a true citizen because of precisely the revelation of the brutally tragic development which pervades the active development of the drama on stage.

The implicitly sacred aspect of great Classical drama, or the like, is that the audience escapes the prison-like domain of rude sense-certainty, for a drama performed among the souls on stage. The unseen spirits of the real persons are materialized, as expressed in the form of the masks worn by souls on stage, all in the domain of the imagination. Yet, that domain of the imagination, is our real world, a domain of immortality, for which that which has the appearance of the flesh is worn as a shadow of reality, a mere mask. On the Classical stage, behind the masks, all souls are immortals, in a domain where mortal passions are the shadows, and the naked souls behind the masks are the reality.

The matter becomes more interesting when we extend such considerations as those to the domain of a physical science consistent with the Classical standpoint of such as Plato, Cusa, Kepler, Leibniz, Riemann, et al. In fact, the required standpoint is that of a physical science of national economy rooted in modern, anti-positivist or other anti-reductionist modes, as in a physical chemistry derived from the implications of Bernhard Riemann's revolution in physical science. The cases of Pasteur, Mendeleyev, Max Planck, Academician V.I. Vernadsky, William Draper Harkins, and Albert Einstein, are typical of this anti-reductionist (e.g., anti-positivist) school of a science of physical chemistry in physical space-time.

The point which I wish to emphasize at this moment, is the crucial role of the scientific imagination. I state that case as follows.

Man in the Mirror of Physical Space-Time

Henceforth, in the remaining portions of this report, we shall treat the domain of presumed sense-certainties, as a special kind of mirror on the wall of history. What that mirror shows us, is not an image of the real universe, but, rather, as Kepler's discovery of universal gravitation demonstrated, it shows us a certain quality of mere shadow of reality projected upon that special kind of image in a mirror which we tend to regard as being what we call the universe of sundry sense-experiences.

Let us name the most crucial of the concepts we must now employ for this purpose, as the notion of *God the Creator* in the image of man as a creative being, as distinct from all other species of existence. This simply means that we are studying the way in which the universe which we inhabit behaves, doing so from the vantage-point of the principled conception of man as made in the likeness of the Creator, a likeness defined by the virtue of our available power of insight into the implications of willful creativity itself. In other words, man, by nature, participates in the quality of willful choice of creating which is otherwise unique to the notion of a willful universal Creator.

Man is not a humble creature from those lower ranks presented to our senses as the Lithosphere and Biosphere. Man is both equipped, by nature, and therefore assigned to participate willfully with the Creator, as Philo of Alexandria rebuked the memory of Aristotle on this account; man is, to participate in the continuing process of universal creation. Man's behavior in the universe is therefore of the nature of a moral obligation to the future. We are designed to contribute, in a participating role, to the perpetual improvement of the universe which we inhabit, to make the universe, and ourselves, better.

V. On the Subject of Creativity

Specifically, our United States of America is now experiencing a kind of process which has been sometimes named "a mass strike." Among the poems which I composed many decades ago, while I was still a young adult, the central topic of a series of such now long-neglected compositions was what I expressed most emphatically in one such case, entitled "My Lyre," by reference to a certain quality of metaphorical ideas which pass like a silent breeze through the universe, "bending stars like reeds." A true "mass strike" is represented essentially by that type of breeze.

At a later point in my historical researches, I considered the related phenomenon of that genius and curiously un-Marxist Rosa Luxemburg's notion of what she named "the mass strike," a concept which no German Social-Democrat or a like breed of avowed "materialist" could ever really understand in a competent choice of ontological terms of reference. In the English literature, good choices of poets considered for comparisons on the premise of this same phenomenon, are poets who are typified best by Keats and Shelley in their time, or, in German, by the sweep of Friedrich Schiller's genius and some of Heine's work, or by Shakespeare earlier. Notably, none of those poets were representative of the world-outlook of the followers of Paolo Sarpi's cult, the reductionist cult of that species of philosophical irrationalism which was the characteristic of British assets of such followers of Adam Smith as Marx and Engels, or the typical Wall Street-owned Liberal of today.

In Rosa Luxemburg's case, her relatively unique genius was expressed in that fact that she was the only relevant political economist of her niche in time who, like that U.S. State Department's historian Herbert Feis who affirmed her definitions in political-economy later, actually understood the actual substance and meaning of the term "imperialism." In fact, only very rare economists still today could present a competent case bearing on this subject-matter.

The only competent approach to removing the mystery from her peculiar competence in the matter of the "mass strike," is what must be presented from the standpoint of the immediately preceding chapter of this report. It is only from this same standpoint, that the revolutionary character of the present global economic crisis can be competently understood. I must, again, emphasize the view of the nature of the human mind which I have introduced in that same chapter. The only appropriate technical term for treating such cases as this one, is Gottfried Leibniz's modern resurrection of the ancient Classical concept of *dynamis* as that principle of *dynamics* which must underlie any serious attempts at treating the specific type of the mass crisis in the U.S.A. and Europe today.

The key for understanding the point I am making here, lies in examining the ontological implications of that concept of the form of the *finite but unbounded* catenary-tractrix function which I have traced, in this present report, from origins located in the interactions between the discoveries for physical science principles represented by the work of Brunelleschi and Nicholas of Cusa, or, later, Johannes Kepler's discovery of the principle of universal gravitation. The argument to be made on that account, runs as follows.

The Sarpian reductionist's misconception of human interrelations is to be traced, usually, from the mistaken view of social relations as expressed primarily in terms of the ontological misconceptions of naive sense-certainty. Already, the ancient Classical conception of *dynamis*, proffered a corrected view of this matter. Archytas' unique solution for the duplication of the cube, was an accomplishment praised highly by Eratosthenes later; it is coherent with the state of organization of the processes of the human mind in which the concept of *dynamis*, or also Leibniz's concept of *dynamics* coheres. Our inner, actual existence, lies not in a scheme consistent with sense-perception; it lies, ontologically, in the domain of physical-space-time for which the sense-perceptual conceptions of the imagined perceptual domain of a separated space, time, and matter, are relatively mere shadows.

Do not be surprised unnecessarily! The real universe is "located" as an expression of relativistic physical-space-time, rather than space, time, and matter. In accord with those facts, let us seek to clarify the apparent paradoxes seemingly posed, by defining two respectively distinct domains, A and B. "A" is the real universe, where the essential actions actually are generated; "B" is the domain of those shadows which are cast upon the seemingly real world of "B" by action located within the real domain of "A."

Again, we must say, that the primary functions of the human mind lie within what the founder of modern dynamics Gottfried Leibniz defined, ontologically, as "the infinitesimal" of his and Jean Bernouilli's calculus, as opposed to the hoax promoted by the frankly silly reductionist, almost positivist mathematician's argument which Liberal convert Leonhard Euler adopted from Abbé Antonio S. Conti's school of Sarpian deceits. Such is the point of clearest separation of a competent physicist, such as Riemann followers Max Planck, Harkins, Vernadsky, and Einstein, from the intrinsically incompetent mere mathematicians of the contemporary positivist schools. There is no actually physical principle adopted among the cults of the positivist school of the heathen followers of Paolo Sarpi and his intellectual offspring of today.[28]

The very fact of the phenomena of "the mass strike" constitutes crucial "experimental" evidence of the nature and effect of the principled distinction of that so-called "mass strike" phenomenon which Percy Bysshe Shelley summarized in the concluding paragraphs of his *A Defence of Poetry*. The principle so expressed also belongs to the category of those systemic forms of Classical irony which are familiar from all great works of artistic composition and the like.

The same principle of irony is also the essential distinction of all competent representation of the appropriate performance of all the competent musical compositions of the Classical composers who followed the model of Johann Sebastian Bach, through

---

28. This is probably best clarified by focussing attention on the positivism of Göttingen's David Hilbert (also a positivist) rather than the utter degenerates, such as that pair of Bertrand Russell devotees Norbert Wiener and John von Neumann, whom Hilbert bounced out of Göttingen on grounds of systemic scientific incompetence.

Describing the political mass-strike process, LaRouche writes that a growing majority of citizens is "now moved to speak with that higher power of the mind which appears to most spectators as 'some miraculous organ,' whose breath 'bends stars like reeds.'" Shown: a three-light-year-tall pillar of gas and dust, in the constellation Carina

Beethoven, Schumann, and Brahms. These works, and their like expressed as principles of poetry and drama, or the only suggested eyes of Rembrandt's bust of Homer contemplating the fatuous Aristotle, are typical of the expressions of true Classical irony which are the hallmark of the creative expressions of the human mind.

The outstanding expressions of those implications are met in the way in which such Classical expressions of true irony may "move" the souls of a mass of the population, as the ordinary citizens of the U.S.A. now express their contempt for, and sense of betrayal by those elected members of Congress whose actions evoke a presently rising tide of rage in the overwhelming majority of the citizens of the U.S.A., and elsewhere, today. It is a growing majority now moved to speak with that higher power of the mind which appears to most spectators as "some miraculous organ," whose breath "bends stars like reeds."

In the prefatory remarks which opened this report, I wrote: "The U.S. economy could be saved, even at this late stage of its perilous decline." It should be clear, in the conclusion of this report, that the entire economy of the planet could also be saved, provided that the U.S. acts appropriately to lead the way. It is less a matter of what you think, than how.

Without Glass-Steagall, America Will Fail

by Paul Craig Roberts

Paul Craig Roberts was Assistant Secretary of the Treasury for Economic Policy under President Ronald Reagan. At Stanford University he was a Senior Research Fellow in the Hoover Institution. At Georgetown University, he held the William E. Simon Chair in Political Economy at the Center for Strategic and International Studies. He has been associate editor and columnist for the Wall Street Journal and columnist for Business Week. He is currently chairman of the Institute for Political Economy.

Paul Craig Roberts

June 9—For 66 years the Glass-Steagall act reduced the risks in the banking system. Eight years after the act was repealed, the banking system blew up, threatening the international economy. U.S. taxpayers were forced to come up with $750 billion dollars, a sum much larger than the Pentagon's budget, in order to bail out the banks. This huge sum was insufficient to do the job. The Federal Reserve had to step in and expand its balance sheet by $4 trillion in order to protect the solvency of banks declared "too big to fail."

The enormous increase in the supply of dollars known as Quantitative Easing inflated financial asset prices instead of the consumer price index. This rise in bond and stock prices is a major cause of the worsening income and wealth distribution in the United States. The economic polarization has undercut the image and reality of the United States as a land of opportunity and has introduced political and economic instability into the life of the country.

These are huge costs, and for the benefit only of the rich, who were already rich.

So, what we can say about the repeal of Glass-Steagall is that it turned a somewhat egalitarian democracy with a large middle class into the One Percent vs. the 99 Percent. The repeal resulted in the destruction of the image of the United States as an open prosperous society. The electorate is very much aware of the decline in their economic situation, and this awareness expressed itself in the last presidential election.

Americans know that the nonsense from the U.S. Bureau of Labor Statistics about a 4.3% unemployment rate and an abundance of new jobs is fake news. The BLS gets the low rate of unemployment by not counting the millions of discouraged workers who cannot find employment. If you haven't looked for a job in the last 4 weeks, you are not considered unemployed. The birth/death model, a purely theoretical construct, accounts for a large percentage of the non-existent new jobs. The jobs are there by assumption. The jobs are not really there. Moreover, the replacement of full time jobs with part time jobs proceeds. Pension and health care benefits that once were a substantial part of the pay package are being terminated.

It makes perfect sense to separate commercial from investment banking. The taxpayer-insured deposits of commercial banking should not serve as backing for investment banking's creation of risky financial instruments, such as subprime and other derivatives. The

U.S. government understood that in 1933, but no longer did in 1999. This deterioration in government competence has cost America dearly.

By merging commercial banking with investment banking, the repeal of Glass-Steagall greatly increased the capability of the banking system to create risky financial instruments for which taxpayer backing was available. So, we have the extraordinary situation that the repeal of Glass-Steagall forced the 99 Percent to bail out the One Percent.

The repeal of Glass-Steagall has turned the United States into an unstable economic, political, and social system. We have a situation in which millions of Americans who have lost full time employment with benefits to jobs offshoring, whose lower income employment in part time and contract employment leaves them no discretionary income after payment of interest and fees to the financial system (insurance on home and car, health insurance, credit card interest, car payment interest, student loan interest, home mortgage interest, bank charges for insufficient minimum balance, etc.), are on the hook for bailing out financial institutions that make foolish and risky investments.

This is not politically viable unless Congress and the President are going to resign and turn over the governance of America to Wall Street and the Big Banks. A growing crescendo of voices is saying that this has already happened.

So, where is there any democracy when the One Percent can cover their losses at the expense of the 99 Percent, which is what the repeal of Glass-Steagall guarantees?

Not only must Glass-Steagall be restored, but also the large banks must be reduced in size. That any corporation is too big to fail is a contradiction of the justification of capitalism. Capitalism's justification is that those corporations that misuse resources and make losses go out of business, thus releasing the misused resources to those who can use them profitably. Capitalism is supposed to benefit society, not be dependent on society to bail it out.

I was present when George Champion, former CEO and Chairman of Chase Manhattan Bank, testified before the Senate Banking Committee against national branch banking. Champion said that it would result in the banks becoming too large and that the branches would suck savings out of local communities for investment in traded financial assets. Consequently, local communities would be faced with a dearth of loanable funds, and local businesses would die or not be born from lack of loanable funds.

I covered the story for *Business Week.* But despite the facts as laid out by the pre-eminent banker of our time, the palms had been greased, and the folly proceeded.

As Assistant Secretary of the U.S. Treasury in the Reagan Administration, I opposed all financial deregulation. Financial deregulation does nothing but open the gates to fraud and sharp dealing. It allows one institution, even one individual, to make a fortune by wrecking the lives of millions.

The American public is not sufficiently sophisticated to understand these matters, but they know when they are hurting. Few in the House and Senate are sufficiently sophisticated to understand these matters, but they do know that to understand them is not conducive to having their palms greased. So how do the elected representatives manage to represent those who vote them into office?

The answer is that they seldom do.

The question before Congress today is whether they will take the country down for the sake of campaign contributions and cushy jobs if they lose their seat, or will they take personal risks in order to save the country.

America cannot survive if excessive risks and financial fraud can be bailed out by taxpayers.

U.S. Representatives Walter Jones and Marcy Kaptur and members of the House and staff on both sides of the aisle, along with former Goldman Sachs executive Nomi Prins and leaders of citizens' groups, have arranged a briefing in the House of Representatives on June 14 about the importance of Glass-Steagall to the economic, political, and social stability of the United States. Let your representative know that you do not want the financial responsibility for the reckless financial practices of the big banks. Let your representative know also that you do not want big banks that dominate the financial arena. Let them know that you want the return of Glass-Steagall.

The effort to reduce the financial risks arising from the commingling of commercial and investment banking by requiring stronger capital positions of financial corporations is futile. The 2007-08 financial crisis required the taxpayers and the printing press and an amount of money that exceeded any realistic capital and liquidity requirements for financial institutions.

If we don't re-enact Glass-Steagall, the risks taken by financial greed will complete the economic destruction of America.

Congress must serve the people, not Mammon.

www.ingramcontent.com/pod-product-compliance
Lightning Source LLC
Chambersburg PA
CBHW081152280526
45787CB00008B/3299